DIVORCE AND DISENGAGEMENT

PATTERNS OF FATHERHOOD
WITHIN AND BEYOND MARRIAGE

EDWARD KRUK

FERNWOOD PUBLISHING • HALIFAX

Editing: Douglas Beall
Cover design: Beverley Rach and Eric Ourique
Design and Layout: Ragland Editing and Design
Printed and bound in Canada.

A publication of
Fernwood Publishing
Box 9409, Station A
Halifax, Nova Scotia
B3K 5S3

Canadian Cataloguing in Publication Data

Main entry under title:

Kruk, Edward.

  Divorce and disengagement

  Includes bibliographical references
   ISBN 1-895686-23-7

1. Divorced fathers. 2. Divorced fathers --
Psychology. 3. Father and child. I. Title.

HQ756.K78 1993   306.874'2   C93-098532-X

•••

Books on men's issues published by Fernwood

Man's Will to Hurt: Investigating the Causes, Supports and Varieties of His Violence, by Joseph A. Kuypers (1992).

Divorce and Disengagement: Patterns of Fatherhood Within and Beyond Marriage, by Edward Kruk (1993).

CONTENTS

List of Tables and Figures

Tables

Figures

Acknowledgements

This book is based on interviews with a number of divorced fathers who generously agreed to be interviewed about their experiences of divorce and the often very painful changes in their relationships with their children. I remain indebted to them for their searching and honest responses, which provided an exceptionally rich source of information.

This project could not have been completed without the financial sponsorship of the National Welfare Grants Directorate, Health and Welfare Canada. I am extremely grateful to them and particularly to Robert Hart for his genuine interest and support.

I would like to thank Dr. Fran Wasoff and Professor Lorraine Waterhouse of the University of Edinburgh, who have contributed in large measure towards the final product. Thanks also to Errol Sharpe of Fernwood Publishing for his always helpful support, Bert Young of John Abbott College for his instructive and cogent commentary on an earlier draft, and Douglas Beall for his meticulous editing of the final manuscript.

Finally, I acknowledge a special debt to Jane Pulkingham, who unfailingly provided a gleam of light throughout the long life of this project and a refuge when sustenance was needed, together with liberal doses of critical commentary. This book is dedicated to her.

Preface

The increase in the rate of divorce during the past quarter century has shifted research interest, therapeutic practice, and social policy attention to a newly emerged population considered to be "at-risk": parents and children affected by marital divorce. The ever expanding divorce literature, a vast array of human service organizations, and legal and policymaking bodies have all clearly identified divorce as a major social phenomenon and mental health issue.

At the same time, fatherhood has been "discovered." The father-child relationship has become a source of considerable public discussion and achieved a high priority for methodological inquiry. An "emergent trend" of more active fatherhood has been identified, which has generated much discussion and controversy in the literature.

This book stands at the interface of current analyses of divorce and fatherhood and engages in a variety of theoretical and practice debates pertinent to both phenomena. Its purpose is to refine current conceptualizations of divorced fatherhood and to provide policymakers, mediators, and family practitioners with an empirically based understanding of the impact of divorce on non-custodial fathers and the now widespread phenomenon of fathers' disengagement from their children after divorce. This book proceeds from the point of view of non-custodial fathers. Their perceptions and stories represent much-needed and important data.

The book presents the results of four years of cross-national research on divorced fathers, which originated from my experience as a social worker in the fields of child welfare, education, and family therapy, with a particular emphasis on work with children and families in the midst of or having gone through the divorce process. The identification of critical mediating factors affecting the outcome of divorce, particularly for children, has remained a lifelong challenge in my work. I have come to recognize the quantity and quality of non-custodial parent-child interaction as a particularly salient factor. Specifically, the absence of the non-custodial father appears to contribute to problematic outcomes for many children of divorce. Over the years, my attempts to engage non-custodial fathers in post-divorce family work have borne fruit. In my clinical practice and my research, I have come to formulate a dramatically different image of these fathers than the stereotype of men largely removed from and disinterested in their children and not significantly distressed after divorce. Without clinical or research literature to demonstrate otherwise, this stereotype is usually left unchallenged. This book represents an effort to identify and integrate the missing elements in the divorce and fatherhood literature. Ultimately, it seeks to challenge prevailing stereotypes and assumptions.

1

Introduction:
Fatherhood and Divorce

Divorce rates have risen dramatically in Canada. For example, the crude divorce rate (defined as the number of divorces each year per 100,000 married people) rose from 54.8 in 1968 to 1,372.2 in 1987 (Statistics Canada 1990). Liberalization of the grounds for divorce in the Divorce Act 1986 resulted in a significant increase in the number of spouses applying under "no-fault" provisions. At the same time, the proportion of women in paid employment has increased markedly from 20 percent of married women with children in the early 1960s, to more than 70 percent today. Women's increased labour force participation and economic independence have significantly challenged traditional ideologies of "motherhood" and are critical factors in the burgeoning divorce rate (Wilson 1991). Patterns of paternal behaviour have also been in flux. An "emergent trend" of "new" fatherhood has been identified, which has generated considerable discussion and controversy in the literature.

As divorce rates continue to rise, the impact of divorce upon family members has become a subject of considerable concern in the clinical, policy, and research realms. The majority of investigators have directed their enquiries to the experiences of mothers, fathers, and children in isolation from each other, and empirical accounts have tended to highlight the sustained negative effects of divorce on the well-being of family members. The identification of factors contributing to positive outcomes has for the most part been lost under the overwhelming mass of data detailing the profound social, emotional, and economic consequences of divorce and the difficult adjustments to these consequences that family members experience. Recent evidence, however, suggests that for the majority of families of divorce, important mediating factors can contribute to positive post-divorce adjustment of family members: (1) the parents' ability to cooperate in their continuing parenting roles, which rests on their ability to reduce conflict and separate their previous marital conflict from their ongoing parental responsibilities, and (2) a consistent and ongoing relationship between children and each of their parents (Wallerstein and Kelly 1980; Hetherington et al. 1978). It has been suggested that a stable post-divorce non-custodial father-child relationship may be the critical factor in the adjustment of *all* family members after a divorce (Hetherington et al. 1976).

Current fatherhood research has demonstrated that despite varying levels of child care involvement, fathers' emotional investment in their children prevails over other aspects of their lives (Cohen 1987), and that fathers' attachment bonds with their children can no longer be regarded as secondary (Lamb 1987; Rutter 1972). Fathers experience significant emotional hardship at the time of divorce and after, particularly if their relationship with their children is perceived as threatened. For fathers, a particularly salient consequence of divorce is the possible loss of one's children. A father's attachment to and involvement with his children earns approval while he is married, and although these feelings of attachment do not cease upon divorce, his ongoing involvement with his children is usually curtailed by traditional custody and access arrangements. Despite legislative and normative changes in the direction of shared parenting, sole maternal custody remains the dominant post-divorce arrangement for families in Canada, with mothers becoming sole custodial parents in 75 percent of all divorce cases, and in 77 percent of legally contested cases (Department of Justice 1990).

Stable and frequent contact rarely occurs between fathers and their children after divorce. The gradual disengagement of non-custodial fathers from participation in the lives of their children is well documented. Recent North American studies have found that more than 50 percent of fathers and children of divorce had *no* contact with each other in the previous year. In a nationally representative sample of U.S. children aged 11 to 16, the last contact with their fathers for 52 percent had been one or more years earlier; only one-third averaged monthly or more frequent contact. More than twice as many children had had no contact with their fathers in the preceding five years as had visited them once a week or more (36 percent versus 16 percent) (Furstenberg et al. 1983).

The process of a father's disengagement from his children typically begins soon after the marital separation and gradually increases over time, most sharply at about twelve months after separation (Hetherington et al. 1978). Between 25-30 percent of children lose contact very soon after the separation (Mitchell 1985). The non-custodial father thus becomes the "missing" father; the "absent father" is a common phenomenon, both physically and economically.

Although divorce has become a central issue for empirical investigation, and researchers and clinicians are increasingly concerned with the antecedents, process, and consequences of divorce, the experience of the non-custodial divorced father has been largely ignored as a legitimate research topic. The lack of empirically grounded studies is particularly striking in light of the growing number of such fathers, and of the amount of research exploring the involvement, attachment, and influence of fathers in two-parent families. Existing studies on divorced fathers have tended either to focus on custodial single fathers or to fail to distinguish between different types of non-custodial fathers, such as those who remain in contact and those who become disengaged from their children's lives.

The reasons for this neglect are varied. The facts that the great majority of custodial parents are female and that fathers are regarded as less central in the post-divorce family contribute to the belief that divorce is significantly more stressful for women than for men, resulting in custodial mothers being more likely than non-custodial fathers to receive attention and support after divorce. The intractable nature of the difficulties experienced by custodial mothers, in the areas of finances, employment, child care, and social isolation are more visible, while the needs of divorced fathers are generally less conspicuous. Though the concept of the non-custodial divorced father is familiar and easily accessible to most, it is often conceptualized in a particular way, with highly negative connotations. Typically, this man is thought of as enjoying his freedom from responsibility after divorce, as dangerous and abusive to his former spouse, and as an inferior caretaker of his children (Foote 1981). Many fathers do not meet their financial child-support obligations, and domestic violence is widespread, yet clearly these phenomena do not reflect the full spectrum of divorced and divorcing fathers.

While non-custodial fathers as a group have been largely underrepresented in research endeavours, virtually absent within the professional literature has been any detailed analysis of *disengaged* non-custodial fathers—that sizeable group who have no contact with their children after divorce. As stereotypes abound with regard to the non-custodial father, the disengaged father is usually assumed to have been minimally involved with and attached to his children, and to lack interest in or a sense of responsibility for their lives. In the absence of any empirical information derived from systematic research, our conceptualization of non-custodial and disengaged fathers is based almost entirely on common stereotypes, which appear to have infiltrated public thinking and the current divorce literature.

The Study

In an attempt to reduce the lacuna in the divorce research literature vis-à-vis non-custodial and disengaged fathers, I embarked on a study of the father-child relationship, examining its various aspects before, during, and after divorce and detailing any changes in the relationship that result from divorce. The main purpose of my research was to further the understanding of service providers and policymakers of the impact of divorce on non-custodial fathers and their disengagement from their children. Through a systematic examination of the characteristics of non-custodial fathers generally, and disengaged fathers specifically, and of their relationships with their children before, during, and after divorce, our understanding of these fathers and how the process of divorce impacts on them as a group can be based on more rigorously gathered empirical information than at present. This information should be of particular value to clinicians, policymakers, and the divorce research community.

In the therapeutic realm, an increasing proportion of clinical caseloads involve parents and/or children presenting at various stages of the divorce process: during the deterioration of the marital relationship, at the time of the decision to divorce, in the period prior to the legal divorce and negotiations over legal terms, during the legal divorce, and during the post-divorce period, including remarriage and step-family formation. Clinicians require empirical data on the effects of divorce on non-custodial fathers so their therapeutic interventions can be relevant both to divorcing families and to the constellation of problems and issues faced by divorced fathers.

As major structural changes within the family have occurred in recent decades, as traditional custody and access arrangements have been increasingly perceived as inadequate, and as conventional methods of child custody and access dispute resolution are called into question, the implications for social policy reformulation are considerable. Family policymakers need empirical data on non-custodial fathers to inform considerations of future policy revision.

My study was thus intended to ground our conceptualization of a population that is familiar but neglected. As recent research on fatherhood in two-parent families has challenged conventional assumptions about the paternal role, so it is hoped that this research, which critically examines prevailing myths and stereotypes, will lead to a clearer empirical grounding of present conceptualizations.

The "Divorced Father"

An important beginning point for a more refined understanding of divorced fatherhood is a re-examination of the term "divorced father." In light of the different patterns of fatherhood within two-parent families, divorced fathers should not be assumed to constitute a homogeneous group, as they are often portrayed. The study sought to sharpen the present focus on the "divorced father" by looking at the dominant form of divorced fatherhood—the *non-custodial* father—and, more specifically, on the absent or *disengaged* father as the prevalent form of non-custodial fatherhood.

The primary objectives of the research were two-fold. First, the more general question of the impact of divorce on non-custodial fathers was examined by empirically and systematically examining the pre- and post-divorce experiences of these men. Second, the research examined why such a high proportion of these fathers disengage from their children's lives after divorce, by comparing the pre- and post-divorce experiences of fathers who remain in contact with their children following divorce with those who have become disengaged. Whereas studies have tended to concentrate on parent-child relationships either within the two-parent family structure or subsequent to divorce, this study explored changes in the nature of the father-child relationship before, during, and after divorce.

Research Design

Surveys were conducted with a sample of eighty non-custodial divorced fathers, half of whom had ongoing and regular contact with their children and half of whom were disengaged with no contact. Contrasting the experiences and responses of fathers who maintain contact with their children following divorce with those who become disengaged is essential in the development of a theoretical understanding of disengagement. Examination of various aspects of the marital and parental experience of "contact" versus "disengaged" fathers allowed the identification of key factors that determine the nature of the father-child relationship after divorce.

A cross-national design was developed for the research. An equal number of Canadian and British fathers were interviewed in the study to allow a comparison of the experiences and responses of non-custodial fathers in two countries. This comparison enabled conclusions to be drawn about non-custodial and disengaged fathers with greater confidence than a study restricted to a single locale would have allowed.

Divorced mothers and other family members were not interviewed. Data was obtained exclusively from the perspective of non-custodial fathers and was compared with existing findings on the impact of divorce on custodial mothers and children. The study proceeded from the assumption that divorced fathers' perceptions in and of themselves, and not previously examined in the divorce literature, represent a legitimate focus for empirical study. Though a relatively abundant body of data has accumulated on the impact of divorce on single custodial mothers and children, research studies that allow fathers to define and expound their own perceptions of their experiences before, during, and after divorce are extremely rare; thus, a case may be made for the validity of such "father-centred" research, where the father's perspective is paramount and his testimony is considered valid for its own sake. However individual definitions and perceptions deviate from "objective reality" (and one may argue that no such reality exists), it is these definitions and perceptions that compose experiences, whether of difficulty or success. One's interpretations of past and current contexts are what one faces and acts upon; thus to study non-custodial fatherhood and disengagement is to treat seriously non-custodial and disengaged fathers' self-reports of their experiences.

Forty of the eighty fathers remained in contact with their children and forty were disengaged, and forty resided in Canada (Metro Toronto and area) and forty in Britain (Edinburgh and area). The final sample was determined according to four basic eligibility criteria established to control for excessive variation and to allow comparison with pre-existing studies of divorce, yet to reflect the actual heterogeneity of the non-custodial divorced father population: (1) the father was to have been separated no more than six years before the interview, (2) to have had no more than two children from the former marriage, (3) with the elder child being under 16 years of age at the time of the interview, and (4) the father was to have neither de facto nor legal custody of the child(ren) of the marriage (the children resided with their mothers, who retained custody in the form of physical care and control).

Though it may be argued that there is no truly random procedure of sampling possible in the case of divorced parents, it was felt, that among the alternatives available, the use of court records to generate a sample would be most likely to result in a wide cross-section of non-custodial fathers representative of the entire population of such men in Canada and Britain. Negotiations were initiated with key officials in the Supreme Court of Ontario and the Scottish Court of Session and Edinburgh Sheriff Court towards access to court records. Negotiations with court officials in Canada presented few difficulties and a procedure for drawing the sample was established; however, access to divorce and interim custody records in Britain was denied. This refusal appeared to be the result of a policy decision on the part of court and government officials to allow access to court records only for government-sponsored and court-sanctioned research projects— ostensibly to limit non-essential demands on court personnel. In the circumstances, we were obliged to adopt the second-best strategy: we recruited divorced fathers from a variety of sources and called a halt when we had obtained the requisite number to generate the British sample.

The source of the data was a structured interview combining fixed-choice and open-ended questions conducted by the researcher individually with each father. A search of the literature revealed no pretested instrument relevant to the particular focus of the present study, although interview schedules of existing studies on divorced fathers and families were screened and provided a useful source of general themes and some questionnaire items. The clinical and "self-help" literature related to divorce was also reviewed; this, combined with the researcher's own experience and professional counselling with intact and divorced families, further guided the identification of salient issues and the construction of the questionnaire.

Data was collected from each respondent by means of an eight-part questionnaire, subsequent to a pretest with a sample of six fathers. Given the desirability of obtaining comparable sets of data from all respondents, the same questionnaire was administered to all respondents. The questionnaire proceeded from an initial focus on demographic data and family history to an increasingly open-ended exploration of various key issues and post-divorce changes in the father-child relationship. It also proceeded according to the time frame of the father's experience—before, during, and after divorce—assuming that there were distinct phases in the divorce process for each individual, each phase with a distinct set of issues:

1. demographic data about the father and the pre- and post-divorce family— information such as age, occupation, and income, sex and age of

children, and a history with respect to the marriage and divorce,

2. descriptive data about the pre-divorce father-child relationship, including the father's involvement with and attachment to his children, as well as information concerning the father's perception of the marriage and his previous "father" role,

3. information about the period during divorce and the father's feelings and experiences during this time—the history of the breakdown of the marital relationship and stresses and conflicts within the marriage, details regarding the decision to divorce and who initiated the divorce, and the events and psychological ambience of the divorce,

4. details regarding the legal aspects of the divorce, including custody, access and financial determinations, and the role of the lawyer throughout the process—the father's experiences with the legal system and the courts, as well as with any other sources of help sought,

5. information about various aspects of the post-divorce experience, with an emphasis on the changing father-child relationship—the current status of the father-child relationship, including level of contact-disengagement, visiting patterns and constraints, and practical aspects such as housing, finances, and employment,

6. data about the physical and mental health effects of the divorce, as well as repercussions on the father's employment,

7. data about changes in the "father" role before and after divorce—designed to measure the father's perception of any change in ten areas of influence which comprise the "father" role, and his degree of satisfaction with this perception, and

8. examination of the major issues identified by the father in relation to his status as a non-custodial parent—allowing the father to speak freely in his own terms about both positive and negative aspects of his relationship with his children after divorce and to identify his perception of the most salient issues confronting non-custodial fathers vis-à-vis their relationship with their children.

The interviews displayed many unique features. Although the interview schedule was designed (and pretested) to be completed within one and one-half to two hours, the interviews in fact lasted on the average between two and two and one-half hours. In the great majority of cases, fathers were willing to share large amounts of intimate, often painfully sensitive information. The rich and extensive information gathered is considered a major strength of the study. For many fathers, the interview represented their first opportunity to discuss their (usually passionate) feelings and experiences related to the divorce in a detailed and thoughtful way. All of the respondents seemed interested in the questions and regarded the venture as a valid one; no father refused to answer a question or failed to treat a point seriously. The interests of both parties coincided around the study: both understood the study as one way to begin to reverse the neglect of non-custodial fathers in the research, clinical, and policymaking realms. The study was seen by the majority of fathers as relevant and useful, and they usually remarked that the questionnaire elicited a fairly complete set of important information. Further, the reciprocal exchange nature of the researcher-respondent contact aided rapport. In exchange for providing the researcher with data, the respondents appeared to take something of value to themselves from the interview: a sense of potentially helping other non-custodial fathers and divorced families, new insights from having reviewed their experiences of divorce, knowledge that others shared their situation, and an opportunity to be heard and have their difficulties validated. Thus the interview contained many therapeutic elements for the fathers who took part.

Characteristics of the Sample

Although two distinct sampling procedures were used in Canada and Britain, both jurisdictions produced a wide spectrum of non-custodial divorced fathers from a variety of backgrounds and with a range of experiences. Safeguards to ensure a representative sample were taken and in large measure were successful in generating a sample reflective of the entire population of non-custodial fathers in both locales.

The eighty fathers were grouped into six occupational class divisions: 15 percent professional, 29 percent intermediate non-manual, 13 percent junior non-manual, 20 percent skilled manual, 17 percent partly skilled manual, and 8 percent unskilled manual workers. The mean age of the eighty fathers at the date of the survey was 39 years and 3 months, and ages ranged from 24 to 56. The former marriage was the first marriage for sixty-nine of the men; eleven had been remarried. The mean length of the marriage to separation was eight years and three months, and lengths of marriage ranged from four months to twenty-four years. Of the eighty separated fathers, thirty-nine were legally divorced, nineteen in Canada and twenty in Britain. Nine had remarried since the divorce, four in Canada and five in Britain. The mean length of the separation at the time of the interview was three years and four months, and length of separation ranged from three months to six years and eleven months. For the thirty-nine fathers who were legally divorced, the mean length of the divorce at the time of the interview was one year and ten months, and divorces ranged from one month to five years and seven months in length. For the nine fathers who were remarried, the mean length of the remarriage was two years and three months, and marriages ranged from one month to five years in length.

The eighty fathers in the sample had a total of 128 children from the former marriage, ranging in age from one to 15 years at the time of the interview. Thirty-two fathers had one child and forty-eight had two children; of the eighty older or only children, forty-two were female and thirty-eight male; of the forty-eight younger children, twenty-five were female and twenty-three male.

2

Patterns of Fatherhood
Within and Beyond Marriage

In his review of theories of fatherhood, Fein (1978) distinguished among three historical conceptualizations or research paradigms: (1) the traditional perspective, prevalent in the 1940s and 1950s, marked by the model of the aloof and distant father who cares for his children primarily by succeeding in the occupational arena, (2) the modern perspective, which characterizes the fatherhood literature of the 1960s, concerned with child outcome variables of sex-role identification, academic achievement, and moral development, all of which may be furthered by paternal involvement, and (3) the emergent or androgynous perspective of the 1970s and 1980s, which explores the premise that men have the capacity to be effective nurturers of their children and to have a wide range of parental skills and interests.

Fathers, like mothers, are highly variable in the enactment of their roles. Many men define themselves in a "traditional" manner and are only peripherally involved in their children's lives, others assume a partial role in child rearing and development, while still others take on the full complement of child care responsibilities. Despite the identification of an "emergent trend" in fatherhood, broad generalizations about fathers that merely assume significant increases in the involvement of men in the home lack credibility; rather, what is needed is a recognition of the heterogeneity of fatherhood and the complexity of the factors and processes that structure the social institution of "fatherhood" and account for existing variations (Segal 1990; Lewis and O'Brien 1987). The father role, both within the two-parent family and after divorce, is enacted within various structural and institutional constraints; fathers' experiences of "fathering" is set within the context of the institution of fatherhood, and within the more general structure of gender-based divisions.

Major structural changes within the family have occurred in recent decades, including declining fertility, rising divorce rates, and the emergence of new family structures. Perhaps most significant, however, has been the rapid influx of married women into the paid labour force; only about 25 percent of North American families now conform to the "traditional" mother-homemaker, father-breadwinner structure (Hanson and Bozett 1985). Women and men are located in both spheres, and their experience of each can be highly interdependent. The "myth of separate worlds" has challenged traditional research paradigms focused either on men in the sphere of employment or women in relation to the family. Feldberg and Glenn (1979) speak of the "work model" for men and the "gender model" for women: men are studied in relation to the "public" sphere of work and politics, with attention focused on variations in their occupational experiences and the manner in which work influences other aspects of their lives; women are examined in relation to the "private" sphere of the family, where family characteristics assume the status of independent variables, and the ramifications for occupational attainment and role conflict are scrutinized. The assumptions underlying such analyses are consistent with traditional gender-based norms: the negative consequences of male *unemployment* for men's families are studied on the one hand, while the deleterious implications of female *employment* for women's families are examined on the other. These assumptions have led researchers to ignore data about men in the family, just as they have traditionally neglected women in the realm of work. Now that a majority of married women are in paid employment, however, there is considerable justification for a new approach: the same conceptual framework should be applied to both men and women in examining links between work and the family. Theories and models that presume that all men are work-centred (the "male-work" model) contribute to the idea that men somehow *ought* to be that way (Mortimer and Sorensen 1984); as Eichler (1983) has argued, "sexist (social) science fails to understand men" because it ignores potential conflicts between men's work and family roles.

Recent research reflects a shift in this traditional paradigm. There is increasing evidence to challenge the stereotype that most men are work- rather than family-oriented. Pleck and Lang (1978) first reported that men's *psychological* involvement with marriage and family is greater than with their work, with family experiences perceived by fathers as making greater contributions to their overall well-being than work outside. This is now widely reported in the literature, most recently by Cohen (1987), who found that fathers' lives contain greater attachments to, and are more profoundly affected by, marriage and fatherhood than is usually assumed, and who called for a rethinking of the nature and depth of men's family roles.

There has been considerable recent discussion about the relationship between maternal employment and paternal participation in family work. In both Britain and North America, labour force participation among married women has grown enormously: in 1986, 62 percent of Canadian husband/wife families with children had two earners, and by 1988, 57 percent of married women with children under age 3 were employed, as were 62 percent with children between 3 and 5, and 70 percent of those with children aged 6 to 16 (Conway 1990). Various investigators have concluded that changes in gender relations have been responsive to changes in female employment (Scanzoni 1979; Pleck 1979; Lamb 1986), while others report a more pessimistic outcome (Benokraitis 1985;

Brannen and Moss 1987). Most agree, however, that the *relative* involvement of men has increased simply because employed women have less time to devote to family work (Lamb 1986; Pleck and Rustad 1980). Pleck (1979) examined data from the 1977 (U.S.) Quality of Employment Survey, a large representative sample, and found that employed husbands averaged a total of 14.5 hours per week on housework and 20 hours per week in child care, as compared with employed wives' totals of 31 hours per week on housework and 33 hours in child care. Employed husbands with employed wives, however, reported spending 1.8 hours per week more in housework and 2.7 hours more in child care than did employed husbands with non-employed wives. Another national time-use study of employed wives in 1976-77 found that wives spent only twelve more minutes a day in *combined* paid work and family work than did their husbands (Pleck and Rustad 1981). More recently, Kamo (1988) found that the work status of both spouses was correlated with their domestic task sharing: while, on the average, husbands carry 36 percent of the total domestic workload (or about half that of their wives), when both work full-time outside the home, this increases to 41 percent, and to 43 percent when both earn approximately the same amount of money. Hochschild and Machung (1989), in an eight-year study of domestic work sharing in dual-earner families, reported 20 percent of couples sharing equally, 70 percent with men doing less than half but more than one-third, and 10 percent in which men continued to perform one-third or less of household tasks. Thus, while there is no question that wives continue to hold the primary responsibility for family work, men's behaviour appears to be changing on an important social indicator: men are beginning to increase their family work, particularly in child-care tasks, when their wives are employed. As the proportion of married women in paid employment continues to grow, fathers' participation in family work may show a corresponding increase (Kamo 1988).

Statistics Canada's 1986 General Social Survey found that Canadian working men spend about two hours a day on domestic work and child care (and they work in paid employment about an hour a day longer than employed women), and working women spend just over three hours. Thus, in Canada the total time invested in paid employment and home and family care by employed men and women is roughly equal (Statistics Canada 1988). Martin and Roberts' (1984) Women and Employment Survey in Britain differentiated between domestic and child care tasks and found that although 44 percent of married women working full-time said they shared *overall* family work (domestic tasks plus child care) equally (as opposed to 23 percent working part-time), 67 percent of these women saw *child care* as shared. In the division of child care tasks, however, mothers were more likely to be involved in routine basic care, such as feeding, dressing, and washing, while fathers spent more time in idiosyncratic play and recreational activities. North American research has revealed a similar pattern, concluding that, within the family, women appear to have "instrumental" roles and men have "expressive" functions: mothers do most of the "routine" child care, and fathers engage more in the pleasurable activities of watching, holding and playing with the child (Coleman 1988; Losh-Hesselbart 1987).

Constraints to Fatherhood within Marriage

Government policy and institutional constraints continue to reflect a gender-based division of labour, providing differential benefits for men and women. In the realm of paid work, most women are restricted to a limited number of occupations, are paid less, and have fewer training and career possibilities; further, the "motherhood mandate" prescribes that they will assume the lion's share of child-care responsibilities. The social construction of fatherhood, in contrast, is such that the "good" male worker "is not expected to let parental commitments influence or interfere with his work. He is expected to follow the same pattern of work, whether or not he has children, a pattern characterized by no breaks in employment, full-time hours and a readiness to work overtime and irregular hours as and when required" (Moss and Brannen 1987:43). The "fatherhood mandate" encourages a consolidation and development of men's position in the realm of employment: material provision is seen as the embodiment of male parenting (Lewis and O'Brien 1987).

Traditional orientations towards "fatherhood" and "motherhood" remain strong despite an increasing heterogeneity of "fathering" and "mothering" roles within families and the fact that men and women are both located in the sphere of employment. Gender-based institutional inequities continue to prevail, and current government policy strongly reflects and reinforces traditional gender stereotypes. The employment and family work patterns of men and women are thus largely determined by realities over which individuals and families have relatively little control: as dominant ideologies and normative constraints limit men's involvement in family work and women's participation in employment, structural barriers restrict their opportunities.

The employment of women with children has become a recognized political issue. The facts that women are found disproportionately in lower paying jobs, with their income being about 67 percent that of men; that labour markets continue to be segmented, with occupational roles largely stereotyped on the basis of gender; that promotion, training, and other opportunities are often unavailable to women; and that the difficulties of combining paid employment with family work commitments largely limit women's occupational choices are now squarely on the public agenda. The employment of men with children, however, is not a public issue to any large degree: it is not recognized in legislation; it is recognized rarely in the employment practices of individual employers; and politically there has been relatively little interest in the subject. In some quarters, however, this lack of attention may be changing as more men are becoming less willing to define personal success solely in terms of occupational and economic success and strive to become more involved with their families (Cohen 1987). The severity of family strains caused by work demands is beginning to be reported. Garnets and Pleck (1979) first described the types of dilemmas men are facing in relation to their children: some men are recognizing that their restricted range of parenting activities causes them to miss significant opportunities for intimacy and satisfaction (role strain); others never experience pleasure because they are constantly vacillating between being rational, respected, and controlling and being available, intimate, and nurturing (role conflict); and other fathers are exhausted from the effort required to satisfy both the "traditional" and "androgynous" role sets (role overload). As most fathers continue to work full-time, they carry the major responsibility for earning income; the assigned role of breadwinner demands the development of occupational skills and long hours away from home. But because men's main interests appear to be shifting to family and child-care tasks, they experience serious role strain and overload, not dissimilar to that experienced by full-time employed mothers (O'Brien 1982). Nearly half the fathers in O'Brien's study expressed high levels of work-home conflict—these men articulated beliefs in shared parenting yet actually did relatively little, while being exposed to heavy employment demands.

The actual amount of time spent working and the scheduling of work are two major constraints consistently identified by working fathers as not allowing them sufficient time with their children (Moss and Brannen 1987; Segal 1990). Cohen (1987), distinguishing between men's reports of their behaviour as fathers and their role attachments, reported that men repeatedly express strong attachments to their identities as fathers, although their opportunities for participation in child care fall far short of their preferred levels of involvement as a result of what they perceive to be unreasonable work demands and the intrusion of their jobs into their family lives. Among the majority of fathers in full-time employment, the evidence points consistently to long hours spent at work; and these hours appear to be longest and the scheduling of work most irregular among fathers of dependent children (Moss and Brannen 1987). It is at the period in the life cycle when many fathers of young children want to become more involved with their family that the family's financial needs are greatest and work is most likely to make excessive demands on their time. Men tend to work longer hours when they have young children, and a significant proportion express high levels of work-home conflict and dissatisfaction over not being able to spend more time with their children and families (O'Brien 1982; Cohen 1987). Overtime and moonlighting are often necessary to supplement family income at the stage of the family life cycle when children are young and family responsibilities are heaviest, a time when career progression considerations are also extremely salient (Lamb et al. 1987). As Veroff and Feld (1970:180) point out, "At this point in the life cycle, work represents their attempt to solidify their career for the sake of their family's security. They are torn between their desire to establish a close relationship with their children and their desire to establish financial security for the family."

As long as gender-based wage differentials and occupational segregation continue to exist, increased paternal family participation may entail a decrease in the family's present and future earning power. A gendered division of labour thus remains intact, even with married women in the paid economy, and with many fathers expressing dissatisfaction with "traditional" roles. Although some families attempt a redivision of labour and status within the family whereby fathers increase their family work responsibilities, conditions outside the family complicate such arrangements. Men are often locked into remaining full-time wage-earners, women's paid work is perceived as subordinate to men's, and men "specialize" in paid work while women "specialize" in family work. Inequality in each sphere feeds into and perpetuates inequality in the other. To break out of this vicious cycle, substantial changes in both the structures of employment and the family are required.

The changing roles of men and women have made the link between work and family explicit: they have revealed how much of what we take as personal is actually social in origin and scope. Efforts to expand options for women and men and to combine paid employment with family responsibilities have made the roles of women (and increasingly men) an intense political issue. The stated non-interference of the government in the "private" realm of the family has been vigorously challenged as state macroeconomic policy, and various public programs have been exposed as key areas of state intervention in the family—all of which serve to reinforce gender-based structures of inequality.

Various studies have pointed out that not all women desire increased paternal participation in child care because it will diminish and perhaps eliminate maternal domination in this domain (Lamb et al. 1987). In the sphere of employment, women remain in lower paid and poorer jobs. Given such continued inequalities, the transformation of men into competent and involved parents may well be perceived as a threat: What areas will be left in which women can excel and derive meaning? (Lewis and O'Brien 1987). Lamb et al. (1987) caution about the effects of increased paternal participation in infant and child care in two-parent families: paternal involvement *can* have positive consequences, but only when it is in accord with the desires of both parents. Children tend to do best when their parents are able to organize their lives and responsibilities in accordance with their own values and preferences, rather than in accordance with a rigid, socially determined pattern. Fein (1978) stresses that any policy to develop men's opportunities to participate in family life should also be concerned with supporting women in paid employment. LaRossa (1988) stresses that individualistic solutions that see the problem of unequal parental participation in child care and child rearing as a "private" matter are highly inadequate—male parenting should be approached as a public issue, because there are significant structural constraints to men's involvement with their children.

Constraints to Fatherhood beyond Marriage

The maintenance of traditional roles and relationships is an integral part of a conservative agenda. The persistence of occupational segregation and wage differentials between men and women is testimony to powerful vested interests. Employers have benefitted from women's lower wages and from men's investment in work. Legislation that promotes changes in gender relations is a clear threat to those invested in the status quo. Eliminating employment discrimination would require an accommodation of employment to the requirements of family life, rather than leaving family life to be changed by the requirements of employment. Such changes threaten the basic organization of the prevailing structure of inequality and cannot be accommodated without public and political action that involves the state and its potential power over the economy and conditions of work, and an intrusion into "private" labour markets.

The equalization of parenting between men and women is thus highly problematic. The interpenetration of work and family is such that to alter power and psychological structures in the family necessitates a concomitant restructuring of power and ideology in the spheres of employment and politics.

The law as an institution of interventive control has traditionally defined the basic rights and obligations of men and women, and fathers and mothers, on the basis of gender, maintaining a sex-based division of family roles and responsibilities and legitimizing structures of inequality in the family and in employment. The law sanctions and reinforces traditional family roles within the two-parent family and upon divorce. Its influence works through prescriptions and proscriptions, incentives and disincentives, that reinforce the primacy of paid work for men and family work for women. Upon divorce, the gender-based division of labour with respect to the care of children is clear: the father continues to be responsible for their economic support, the mother for their care. The mother is considered the appropriate custodial parent, the father becomes the non-custodial parent. Thus we see a consistent pattern of decisions that justify and reinforce a maternal presumption; this judicially constructed preference has operated as effectively as a statutory directive, sanctioning and preserving fundamental gender-based inequalities in the post-divorce family.

Egalitarian parenting between fathers and mothers in two-parent families and shared custody arrangements after divorce are novel phenomena representing the "private" solutions of families to the problems of gender-based inequality and the role overload of women and men who combine paid work with family work responsibilities. These types of arrangements put pressure on political, economic, and social structures for necessary changes, such as parental leave, leave for family reasons, flexible working schedules, job sharing, freely available child-care facilities, and the elimination of gender-based inequities in the workplace— and thus represent a clear threat to the prevailing structure of inequality. Shared parental custody after divorce threatens men's occupational roles, and the notion of a father as the custodian of his children threatens the normative order. Whereas sole maternal custody is seen to fit the social role of fathers and the time allocation required for their occupational role, shared custody, with its greater involvement of men in child care and rearing, would require a radical shift in values, a reordering of gender relations, and increased political and social supports.

The judicial system has a crucial role to play in limiting child custody and access options, maintaining and legitimizing traditional structures and relationships, and perpetuating gender-based inequalities after divorce. Upon divorce, the judicial system diverts attention from such inequalities by "individualizing" an essentially structural problem, obscuring the need to alter employment structures to make them compatible with family life. Deflecting attention from the wider structural issues of the inferior economic position of women and the need to provide expanded role options for women and men (employment equity, the involvement of men in child care and child rearing, and improved state benefits for families), the law deals with the negative consequences of divorce on family members by focusing on the enforcement of financial support payments. It legitimizes the call for solutions on an individual level. Women's traditional economic ties to and dependence on their former husbands are thereby perpetuated, as are traditional family structures and gender relations.

In sum, the impact of structural factors on post-divorce father-child relationships is clear. To ensure that the "motherhood/fatherhood mandate" remains intact after divorce, responsibility for child care after divorce is fully invested in the mother. The law also influences ideology and belief systems. In its appropriation of post-divorce child custody and in its access determination, the law limits post-divorce options for families and provides notions of appropriate work and family role behaviours. Sole maternal custody with limited paternal access (and paternal responsibility for financial provision) thus comes to be perceived as the only available option for divorcing families. Thus, in approximately 75 percent of all cases, and 77 percent of contested cases, fathers become non-custodial parents, and "there has been no appreciable or consistent change in the basic patterns of awarding sole custody since at least the early 1970's" (Department of Justice 1990:133).

The fact that patriarchal social structures continue to bestow power and privilege upon men in several realms is beyond dispute; the price that men are paying for these privileges is often less emphasized. In the realm of divorce in particular, as men's emotional ties to their families take precedence over their work roles, the costs of male privilege in employment and political stuctures are beginning to surface.

Profile of Fathers in the Study

Fatherhood before Divorce[1]

Like other recent empirical investigations that point to a heterogeneity of fathering roles (Lewis and O'Brien 1987; Lewis and Salt 1986; Hanson and Bozett 1985), the fathers in this study were highly variable in their descriptions of their pre-divorce family roles and relationships: some defined themselves in a traditional manner, as contributing to the family primarily in an economic sense and only being minimally involved in child care and domestic responsibilities; others saw themselves as contributing as caregivers in only certain defined areas;

and yet others saw an active child-care role as an important component of their identity and a significant factor in their everyday lives. Three aspects of reported pre-divorce fathering were distinguished: participation in child care and child rearing tasks, attachment to and emotional investment in children, and perceived influence in children's growth and development. These were then compared to fathers' stated ideologies regarding fatherhood.

Paternal involvement in child care and child rearing was examined in two areas: fathers' participation in a range of infant care tasks relative to their wives' involvement, and the actual amount of fathers' weekly contact with their children, both alone and with others, in the year before the separation/divorce. Fathers' participation in infant care tasks relative to their wives' involvement was highest in playing with the baby (50 percent), lulling the baby to sleep (50 percent), and taking the baby for a walk (40 percent), and was lowest in preparing the baby's meals (20 percent) and taking the baby to the doctor or caring for when ill (20 percent). These findings reflect earlier research that highlighted the selective nature of paternal involvement in child care, with higher reported levels of paternal involvement in idiosyncratic play with children in comparison to routine physical care (Jump and Haas 1987). Reported levels of infant care varied widely across the sample. Importantly, fathers' self-reports were well within the range reported in current studies of husbands' relative participation in family work tasks (36 percent in Kamo [1988]; and 40 percent in Warner [1986]).

Fathers' involvement with their children as the children grew older was also examined. Fathers were asked to indicate the actual amount of time they spent in direct contact with their children per week, both alone and with others present, in the year before the divorce. The fathers' overall level of involvement was reported to average thirty-four hours per week, of which sixteen hours were time spent alone with the children. Again, considerable variation was evident.

Consistent with earlier findings, the fathers in the sample described themselves as highly emotionally attached to their children during the marriage, whether or not they had been actively involved in child care. They generally reported high affective involvement with their children during the marriage, despite widely varying levels of physical caretaking and time spent with their children, supporting current research findings which cast men in more affective poses than thought previously. Fathers' attachment to their children in relation to other role attachments was also measured. Although their behaviour may suggest that their occupational role is primary (based on the relative amount of time invested), fathers overwhelmingly reported deriving greater satisfaction from their family and children than from their work or other roles.

Children are salient individuals in their fathers' lives, and recent research has emphasized the importance of fathers in the lives of their children. Ten categories of parental functions were examined that together can be considered as comprising the "father" role (Greif 1977); these were used in the present study to assess the nature of fathers' influence on their children's lives before divorce (see Table 1 page 24).

Table 1. Perceived Paternal Influence on Children Before Divorce

Paternal Roles	Very High/High %(N)	Medium %(N)	Low/very Low %(N)	No Influence %(N)	Total %(N)
Routine daily care and safety	74(59)	16(13)	9(7)	1(1)	100(80)
Intellectual development	74(59)	19(15)	5(4)	3(2)	100(80)
Physical development	74(60)	14(11)	10(8)	1(1)	100(80)
Personality development	76(61)	19(15)	4(3)	1(1)	100(80)
Teaching Behaviou/social skills	78(62)	19(15)	4(3)	—	100(80)
Emotional development	68(54)	20(16)	11(9)	1(1)	100(80)
Religious development	39(31)	26(21)	20(16)	15(12)	100(80)
Moral development	68(54)	21(17)	9(7)	3(2)	100(80)
Giving child(ren) a feeling of being part of a family	78(62)	15(12)	6(5)	1(1)	100(80)
Financial affairs of child(ren)	54(43)	38(30)	8(6)	1(1)	100(80)

Fathers generally perceived their pre-divorce influence in various dimensions of their children's growth and development to have been high, particularly in giving their children a "feeling of being part of a family" and in "teaching behaviour and social skills," and generally lower in the "religious development" and "financial affairs" of their children. Significantly, fathers saw themselves as having had a strong influence in their day-to-day interaction with their children. Again, there was considerable variation among fathers' in their stated levels of influence in most categories.

In addition to measuring fathers' reported levels of (behavioural) involvement in child-care and child-rearing functions, emotional attachment to their children, and influence on their children's lives, indices of fathers' attitudes and ideologies regarding gender role division within the family were developed to provide further information about the pre-divorce father-child relationship. In this regard, fathers were asked to provide a definition of "mothering," "fathering," and "family life," and to indicate their major strengths and weaknesses as parents during the marriage and their views of the differences between the "mother" and "father" roles in the family. In regard to the latter, fathers' replies fell broadly into the categories shown in Table 2, indicative of an heterogeneity of attitudes and orientations towards gender role division within the family:[2]

Table 2.   Fathers' Ideologies Regarding Gender Roles

	% (N)
No difference between "father" and "mother" role in family ("androgynous" orientation)	66(53)
Some difference between "father" and "mother" role in family ("mixed" orientation)	8(6)
Fundamental difference between "father" and "mother" roles in family ("traditional" orientation)	26(21)
Total	100(80)

The majority of fathers (66 percent) indicated that they believed there is no fundamental difference between the father and mother roles in the family, and 26 percent indicated that they perceived the two roles to be distinct and complementary. Significantly, fathers' reported ideologies closely matched their reported rates of involvement with, attachment to, and influence on their children before divorce. Fathers who reported high levels of involvement, attachment, and influence consistently provided responses that indicated an "androgynous" orientation towards gender roles within marriage.

Although one must proceed with caution in any interpretation of the above data because of the retrospective and self-report nature of the study, the results closely correspond to those of existing studies of fatherhood in two-parent families. For the fathers in our study, a clear heterogeneity of fathering roles existed before divorce . The primary reason for assessing the quality of father-child relationships prior to divorce was to determine what, if anything, the father and child were losing upon divorce. The loss of a highly attached, close-knit relationship has a radically different meaning than one in which the father had only been peripherally involved with his children during the marriage.

During Divorce

Fathers were asked what they perceived to be the main factors that contributed to the divorce. Consistent with earlier studies (e.g., Ambrose et al. 1983), in the great majority of cases, difficulties with the children or child rearing were not cited as contributing factors in the parents' divorce (see Table 3).

Table 3.   Reasons for Divorce

Nature of Reason	Reason 1 %(N)	Reason 2 %(N)	Total %(N)
Internal to the marriage and concerning the relationship between the couple alone	53(42)	16(6)	41(48)
Internal to the marriage but concerning the couple and their children	4(3)	16(6)	8(9)
Relationship by one or both of the spouses with another or others	10(8)	16(6)	11(14)
Tensions related to work or career (of either spouse) or money matters	14(11)	32(12)	19(23)
Pressures from in-laws and other extended family	11(9)	13(5)	11(14)
Illness of either spouse	9(7)	8(3)	8(10)
Totals	100(80)	100(38)	100(118)

Classification of nature of reasons based on Ambrose et al. (1983).

When asked about the general atmosphere between the spouses at the point of the divorce (i.e. final parental separation), somewhat surprisingly, fathers were more likely to report an atmosphere of calm (44 percent) than of turbulence (35 percent). Many indicated a limited level of awareness of the impending divorce; twenty-one fathers stated that they experienced the divorce as caused by a particular event or crisis (rather than as a slow build-up) for which they were largely unprepared, reflecting a lack of awareness of serious conflicts or chronic problems within the marriage.

Consistent with current trends (Statistics Canada 1989; Ambrose et al. 1983) , in the majority of instances (fifty-four of eighty, or 68 percent), the wife was identified as initiating the divorce; the husband was the initiator in only eighteen cases; and it was a mutual decision in eight instances. In fifty-eight of the sixty-four wife- or mutually initiated separations, the husband indicated that he had not wanted the separation to occur; thus only thirty-two of the eighty fathers (40 percent) indicated that they had wanted the separation or made the decision to separate. In most cases (fifty-three of eighty, or 66 percent) there had been only one separation; there had been two in twenty-two cases and three or more in only five instances. In forty-one of the fifty-two attempted reconciliations, the husband had initiated the attempt. Many fathers saw themselves as having little power or control at the time of the divorce over the eventual outcome and expressed a sense of a victimization as unwilling partners in the break-up. Thus despite fathers' reports of an apparent calm between the spouses at the point of the divorce, considerable disagreement over the fact of the divorce itself was predominant.

Further issues where overt or covert disagreements appeared occurred at the time of the divorce, specifically those concerning child custody and access (see Figure 1). Custody disagreements were invariably associated with disagreements over access. Disagreements over custody and access were more likely in wife-initiated divorces; disagreement over the fact of the divorce were usually accompanied by disagreements over custody and access, with fathers wanting to remain actively involved with their children while their wives were reported as wanting a "clean break." Such disagreements were reported as less likely in cases where the husbands had made the decision to divorce; these fathers were more likely to consent to their wives' proposed arrangements (see Tables 4 and 5). Disagreements over both property settlement and support payments, in contrast, were not significantly affected by who initiated the divorce.

Figure 1.   Issues of Disagreement between Spouses at the Time of Divorce

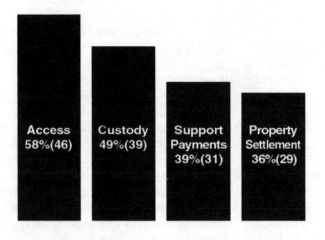

| Access 58%(46) | Custody 49%(39) | Support Payments 39%(31) | Property Settlement 36%(29) |

Table 4.   Custody Disagreement by Initiator of Divorce[3]

| Initiator of Divorce | Custody Disagreement | | |
	Yes %(N)	No %(N)	Total %(N)
Husband or mutual agreement	13(5)	51(21)	33(26)
Wife	87(34)	49(20)	68(54)
Total	100(39)	100(41)	100(80)

p<.001

Table 5.   Access Disagreement by Initiator of Divorce

Initiator of Divorce	Access Disagreement		
	Yes %(N)	No %(N)	Total %(N)
Husband or mutual agreement	20(9)	50(17)	33(26)
Wife	80(37)	50(17)	68(54)
Total	100(46)	100(34)	100(80)

$p < .01$

After Divorce

The most salient feature of fathers' post-divorce experiences was the desire for a higher level of contact with their children. Seventy percent (fifty-six) of fathers indicated a wish for "a lot more" contact with their children than they actually had. This desired level of contact was significantly related to who had initiated the divorce; wife-initiated divorces were strongly associated with fathers' subsequent desire for greater contact with their children.

Fathers were asked about the influence of their ex-wives on the level of the father's contact with his children after divorce. Encouragement of contact by the former spouse after the divorce was also significantly related to the initiator of the divorce. Although most ex-wives discouraged paternal contact (fifty-four of eighty, or 68 percent), those who had initiated their divorces were reported as more likely to discourage it (forty-one of fifty-four, or 76 percent). Predictably, it was found that the greater the discouragement of paternal contact by the former spouse, the more likely the father was to desire greater contact.

The ways in which ex-wives discouraged contact varied, but most often cited were denial of access (mentioned twenty-five times); not having the children ready or available for the access visit, or changing arrangements at the "last minute" (sixteen); confrontation or conflict with the father at the time of the access visit (sixteen); criticism of the father to the children (fifteen); and periodic refusal of access or refusal of residential access (thirteen).

Interestingly, however, whether or not a father actually maintained contact with his children after divorce was largely independent of who had initiated the divorce.

Again, the lack of corroborative data from mothers and children on post-divorce patterns and events is a serious limitation of the study. However, the fact that the most salient feature of the post-divorce experience for fathers was their

3

The Grief Response of Non-Custodial Fathers: Child Absence, Role Loss, and the "Visiting" Relationship

For the great majority of fathers, divorce presents a strain very different than that on mothers: the actual or potential loss of custody of one's children. Burgess et al. (1971) asserted that "in cases where children are present, the parent who retains the children experiences less crisis than the one who is cut off from both the former mate and the children." Ambert (1980) corroborates this assertion, stating that parents with custody of their children generally experience less change in their living situation, feel less lonely, insecure, and helpless in their relationships with their children, and have "an entrance into a better regulated emotional reality" than parents without custody.

About the divorced father, Kressel (1980) writes, "most importantly, as the non-custodial parent he must adapt to seeing his children less frequently and often on a schedule not of his own choosing. His lessened involvement in his children's lives combined with the children's lessened involvement in his life may occasion an extremely painful and continuing emotional injury." One of the divorced father's greatest post-divorce tasks is to redefine his role as "parent." Father-child relationships after divorce are especially problematic because the non-custodial situation has no counterpart and therefore no model within the family. "The parent who moves out of the household begins a new role for which there is no dress rehearsal and no script . . . a visiting relationship between parent and child is strange by its very nature" (Wallerstein and Kelly 1980). There is little formal assistance available to help fathers to learn what their new role entails and how they might exercise it in the best interests of their children.

Several factors influence the nature of the post-divorce non-custodial father-child relationship. Non-custodial fathers experience an abrupt disentanglement from their previous parenting role. The everyday routines and events of family life are suddenly replaced by the patterns and constraints of a "visiting" relationship, if not complete cessation of contact (Wallerstein and Kelly 1980). Fathers acutely fear losing their relationships with their children (Jacobs 1986a), which often leads the non-custodial father to play what is referred to as a "Santa Claus" role: visits often involve entertainment and gifts and the father is generally unwilling to discipline his children (Wallerstein and Kelly 1980; Hetherington et al. 1978).

Difficulties surrounding paternal "visitation" have been highlighted by Wallerstein and Kelly (1980). The fact that the "visits" are constrained by time and location tends to create an artificial atmosphere. Feelings and needs are compressed into the narrow confines of a visit, time becomes a jarring presence, and the anxiety of parting constantly looms. Children's upset when they have to say goodbye at the end of a visit often invokes guilt and pain in fathers. Lund (1987) found that fathers who experienced visits as painful for themselves also saw the visits as painful for their children.

In her study of non-custodial fathers, Greif (1979:313) observed that fathers' perceptions of their degree of paternal influence is dependent on the amount of contact between their children and themselves and that "child absence" can have disastrous effects:

> The greater the father's involvement with his child, the greater his sense of having an ongoing parental role in the child's life after divorce. Most importantly, this becomes self-reinforcing: the more opportunity fathers have to act as fathers, the more they see themselves as fathers and seek to continue that involvement. ... On the other hand, the less opportunity fathers have to act as fathers, the less they see themselves as fathers and, ultimately, the less they are motivated to be with their children. A clear danger of child absence is perceived role loss, leading to further withdrawal from the child.

Greif echoes Merton's (1968) assertion that role loss can lead to retreatism. Infrequent visiting, contributing to fathers' feelings of a lack of influence, control, and importance with their children may result in less frequent visiting and, for some, a cessation of parenting altogether. The fathers who experienced more of Greif's "child absence" manifested greater signs of depression, including a depressed mood and difficulty sleeping, eating, working and socializing. These fathers were overwhelmed by feelings of loss for their children and by a sense of devaluation as parents. Hetherington et al. (1978) found that the most compelling problem for divorced fathers is their pervasive sense of loss of their children: eight of the forty-seven fathers in their study who had been highly involved, affectionate parents while married reported that they could not tolerate the pain of only intermittently seeing their children. Two years after the divorce, these fathers had diminished the frequency of their visits with their children. Wallerstein and Kelly (1980) found that non-custodial fathers who experienced feelings of depression, guilt, or anger carried internal barriers that often discouraged visiting. Dealing with their own emotional reactions to the divorce as they simultaneously attempt to play a fuller parenting role is a major difficulty for non-custodial fathers in the first months following divorce. Complicating their situation is the need to deal with their ex-wives in arranging visits. Several authors point to the highly emotionally charged nature of these exchanges and suggest that the stress of receiving and returning children to the former spouse inhibits the amount of contact for many fathers (Hetherington et al. 1978; Greif 1979; Wallerstein and Kelly 1980).

Fathers' abilities to maintain the sense of an ongoing parental role is strongly affected by their feelings of helplessness in overcoming a custodial mother's opposition to visits (Lund 1987). In their study of divorced fathers, Ambrose et al (1983) found that most identified the lack of confirmation of their role as fathers by their ex-wives and their ex-wives' families as the major reason for their loss of contact with their children. Mothers' denial of paternal access to children, however, may, in some cases, be a response to a history of spousal or child abuse that may have led to the divorce. Separated and divorced women are much more likely to have been abused than married women. In Canada, fifty-five of every thousand separated women (as opposed to two of every thousand married women) were subject to physical and/or sexual assault by their spouses (Conway 1990).

Hetherington et al. (1978) reported that two-thirds of the contacts between ex-spouses two months after separation were marked by acrimonious disagreements over access, support, and child-rearing practices. Wallerstein and Kelly (1980) reason that when contacts with the former spouse are aversive, non-custodial fathers become discouraged in their attempts to maintain a relationship with their former families and rapidly lose contact with their children.

Various clinical accounts have identified the "struggle for parental identity" as characteristic of the post-divorce process for many families (Jacobs 1986a; Williams 1983). This struggle may become so intense that each parent seeks to bolster his or her parenting role by devaluing and invalidating the other's. In the extreme, "psychological erasure" of one of the parents can become a real or imagined threat, especially for fathers. If the threat is real, fathers are often rendered helpless and hopeless in their struggle for parental identity; fathers usually give up and withdraw, or fight ferociously to maintain their parental identity (Williams 1983).

Incompetence in the primary caretaker role has also been identified as a major initial difficulty for non-custodial fathers (Hetherington et al. 1978). After divorce, many fathers feel overwhelmed by the multiple nature of the full caretaking role, even on a part-time basis; feelings of incompetence in meal planning and preparation, laundry, housecleaning, and the like add to the difficulty of the visitation-based father-child relationship. Another frequently mentioned problem is providing a home or homelike environment in which children can be with their father and the related difficulties of the children's preferences or needs for certain foods, toys, and clothes to be available (Wallerstein and Kelly 1980). In regard to child management skills, Hetherington et al. (1978) found that divorced fathers of preschool-age children made fewer maturity demands, communicated less well, were less affectionate, and were markedly less consistent in discipline and control of children than fathers in intact families. Wallerstein and Kelly (1980) have suggested that attending to children's emotional needs is especially difficult for non-custodial fathers because of communication skills deficits, the father's own heightened emotional tension, and the nature of the visits themselves, which forestall the intimacy necessary for meeting a child's emotional needs. Related to this, fathers of more than one child are faced with the difficulty of finding time to attend to each child's needs on a one-to-one basis.

Mental, Physical, and Emotional Health

Several studies have examined the impact of divorce on men in general in regard to vulnerability to mental illness. Bloom (1975) discovered that divorced men were nine times more likely to be admitted to psychiatric hospitals for the first time than men from intact families (the increase being threefold for divorced women). His data also showed that admission rates were higher for separated than legally divorced men, suggesting that the period around the time of actual separation is critical. Bloom et al. (1978) found that automobile accidents double in frequency from six months before to six months after divorce. Separated and divorced men are also overrepresented in surveys of suicides, homicides, and deaths resulting from illness. The incidence of spousal abuse rises dramatically during and after separation and divorce: 46 percent of wife battering occurs after separation (Corcoran and Melamed 1990), and three-quarters of domestic assaults reported to police occur after separation (Hart 1990).

Jordan (1985) concluded that the most striking effects of divorce for men with children were in the area of mental health: between 60-80 percent of men reported a number of long-lasting stress-related symptoms, such as sleeplessness, crying, reduced energy, poor appetite and excessive tiredness. Ambrose et al. (1983) found that 68 percent of divorced fathers exhibit new mental health problems after divorce, 33 percent of a severe nature. The research literature on non-custodial divorced fathers has documented the following effects of divorce on mental health: loss, grief, and sadness (Greif 1979; Keshet and Rosenthal 1978); loneliness (Wallerstein and Kelly 1980); depression and apathy (Greif 1979; Keshet and Rosenthal 1978; Wallerstein and Kelly 1980); and inadequacy and feelings of incompetence (Hetherington et al. 1978). Studies have also examined the physical health effects of divorce on these fathers. Both Greif (1979) and Ambrose et al. (1983) found that, after divorce, in close to half of their samples, fathers developed physical symptoms, including weight loss, nerve-related eye and dental problems, high blood pressure, increased drinking, sleeping and eating difficulties, and a host of psychosomatic complaints.

The clinical literature has suggested that a primary concern for many divorcing fathers is the threat of losing their relationships with their children.

Fathers frequently perceive divorce as requiring a dramatic diminution or total severance of this relationship (Jacobs 1986a). In the psychiatric literature on divorce, "involuntary child absence syndrome" has been identified and defined as the "group of symptoms, feelings, ideas and behaviour that are precipitated in some parents during or following separation or divorce when they are threatened with, feel threatened by, or must in fact live with a non-existent, minimal, or diminished relationship to one or more of their children" (Jacobs 1986a). Jacobs' study of twenty-six divorcing and divorced fathers in psychiatric treatment showed these men to be preoccupied by their sense of impending loss.

Fathers of infants and young children have been identified as a group who may be particularly devastated by the loss of contact with their children, which indicates close attachment bonds and may represent a positive change from gender-based stereotyping (Huntington 1986). Another high-risk group identified by Huntington comprises fathers who know themselves to have been the warmer, more nurturant parent for their children, but who are unable to remain in contact on more than a "visiting" basis. As with Jacobs' (1986a) findings, Huntington's conclusions are substantiated only by clinical observations of a limited number of fathers seen in professional practice.

Despite the fact that divorce is a highly stressful event for fathers, dramatically increasing the incidence of emotional, mental, and physical health problems, few avail themselves of traditional clinical resources and most tend to avoid professional contacts (Jacobs 1986a). Jordan (1985) found that more than half of the men in his sample who exhibited severe symptoms sought no help at all.

Several researchers (Scher 1981; Chiriboga et al. 1979) have highlighted the fact that men's difficulties in accepting help mainly result from the traditional role behaviours ascribed to them, of not admitting problems to others, being in control of their lives, and hiding vulnerable feelings. Others (Jordan 1985; Ambrose et al. 1983) have suggested that traditional clinical services are rarely geared to men's needs and therapeutic agents often lack a basic understanding of the significance of divorce for fathers.

Interpersonal Relationships

The theme of the social isolation of divorced fathers is recurrent in the professional literature. Generally speaking, as their former social network often collapses, divorced fathers rarely have a sympathetic support system, and they experience serious difficulties in socializing and establishing new relationships (Greif 1979; Hetherington et al. 1978). White and Bloom (1981) concluded that the most common source of difficulty for all divorced men is in the area of social behaviour. Social isolation or rapid reattachment are common patterns of behaviour for the recently divorced; loneliness is a pervasive problem and is highly predictive of poor overall adjustment; and social contacts outside the marriage prior to separation appear to be of major help in men's post-divorce adjustment—those who had not been totally dependent on their wives for social activities while married and had a social life independent of the marriage adapt more successfully after divorce (Bloom et al. 1979). Raschke (1977) and Hetherington et al. (1978) found that involvement in new social networks and activities was correlated with positive outcomes for divorced men. Most common in the case of divorced fathers, however, is a general movement towards self-sufficiency and isolation, which continues for a considerable time after divorce (Ambrose et al. 1983). The crisis of divorce and confusion about relating to people in general results in the majority of fathers experiencing negative feelings about themselves and a serious loss of self-esteem, and their trust in others becomes severely depleted (Jordan 1985).

In regard to the effects of divorce on fathers' work and career, financial position, and general living situation, some investigators (White and Bloom 1981; Greif 1979) have detected a strong relationship between poor adjustment to divorce and poor work performance and absenteeism; while others (Hetherington et al. 1978) highlight a pattern among divorced men of spending longer hours at work and less at home, enabling them to better their economic situation and avoid returning to the solitude and inactivity of an empty house. A number of studies have indicated that divorced fathers generally experience increased financial burdens after divorce (Bloom et al. 1979; Hetherington et al. 1978) and a notable decline in their standard of living (Ambrose et al. 1983; Wallerstein and Kelly 1980).

Positive Aspects

There appears to be an increasing confluence of thought within the literature that fathers who maintain regular, ongoing contact with their children make the best transition to the post-divorce period (Hetherington et al. 1978; Wallerstein and Kelly 1980; Jacobs 1986a). The impact of divorce may act as a causal factor in changing men's conceptions of masculinity and helping them to expand the nature of their involvement with their children (Huntington 1986). Some divorced fathers may be "part-time" fathers and yet feel closer to their children and more knowledgeable about them than when they lived together on a full-time basis. A number of men develop stronger ties to their children than they had before divorce, being more likely to spend time together alone, in more intense and meaningful ways (Keshet and Rosenthal 1978). Friedman (1980) points out the positive effects of divorce on the father's experience as a parent: the opportunity exists for "increased nurturing experience" and greater intuitive appreciation of a child's growth and development.

Greif (1977) found that 45 percent of the fathers in her sample reported that divorce had actually brought them closer to their children. Satisfaction with the post-divorce father-child relationship was seen to be associated with satisfaction with the custody arrangement, amount of time spent with the children, and current degree of influence in the children's growth and development.

Hess and Camara (1979) contrast "Santa Claus" fathers with those whose residence becomes the children's second home. In the latter situation, children are fully integrated into the household routine as family members rather than "guests," providing both father and children with ample opportunity for informal interaction. Keshet and Rosenthal (1978) also differentiate between fathers whose visits with their children are dominated by frenetically programmed activity and those who provide a more "homelike" pace and atmosphere. The latter group are able to successfully create their own households and set up schedules for frequent contact with their children, and their initial feelings of inadequacy, anxiety, and depression are gradually replaced by a sense of confidence and accomplishment.

The clinical and research literature, however, indicates that for the majority of divorced fathers, life after divorce is far from a positive experience. Although much of the literature lacks an empirical approach and often relies on autobiographical accounts, clinical observations and reports, and self-selected samples, the notion that fathers have little difficulty adjusting to divorce has been strongly challenged. Available research evidence indicates that the majority of divorced fathers experience stress severe enough to bring on new physical and mental health problems and to create serious relationship difficulties.

Grief Response of Non-Custodial Fathers in the Study

Before their divorces, the non-custodial fathers interviewed played a variety of roles when it came to child-care tasks and had a variety of perceptions and ideologies regarding gender relations in the family. At the same time, fathers had a large emotional investment in their children, describing themselves as strongly attached to their children and as highly influential in their lives. The period during divorce is the time when new father-child relationship patterns are established and consolidated; fathers' involvement with their children after divorce, however, largely falls short of desired levels.

The first main finding of the study was that, upon divorce, non-custodial fathers experience a grieving process that contains all of the major elements of bereavement and is directly and primarily linked to the loss of the pre-divorce father-child relationship. Although non-custodial fathers undergo a number of transitions during divorce, the loss of the pre-divorce father-child relationship is identified by fathers as the most salient, and it is the recognition of this loss that appears to initiate a process of mourning. Non-custodial fathers who are able to establish a new relationship with their children in the critical period during divorce are, for the most part, able to come to some resolution of their grief; those who are unsuccessful in doing so, however, face pronounced ongoing difficulties.

Individual fathers' adaptations to the consequences of divorce range across a continuum, from those who are able to successfully negotiate terms of custody and access and go on to establish a new relationship with their children within the confines of "visiting," to those who are unable to cope with the reality of the loss of the old relationship and fail to set about making a "new start." Each father's response across the continuum is unique, but there are common threads. For the majority of non-custodial fathers, the experience of divorce eventuates a process of bereavement: an upheaval of one's pattern of life, a searching for the lost child, anger and outbursts of rage, despair and an overwhelming sense of loss, but the finality of death is absent. Fathers described confused and frightened reactions as characteristic of the first stages of divorce, in respect to their relationships with their children and with other people. Then came feelings of anger, bitterness, and frustration, usually directed towards the former spouse, and often resulting from legal negotiations regarding custody and access or unsuccessful attempts to maintain contact with one's children. Finally, pervasive feelings of sadness, a sense of loss, loneliness, hopelessness, and depression.

> As far as what fathers themselves go through, I'd read the Elizabeth Kubler-Ross book on the five stages of dying, and I'd noticed along the way that I was going through the same stages—disbelief, a lot of anger, grief—I've had a lot of that, a lot of crying, and then resignation, acceptance. Now, death is a great stress situation, but the break-up of a family can be a type of death, it can be similarly stressful. Some people may be bloody glad, they may feel relief after separation—but it can also be, for others, the most stressful event in their lives. And I think the same five stages apply not just to dying, but to any great stress situation, including the breakdown of a family. (Canadian "contact" father).

Wiseman (1975) outlined a grief process of divorce that builds upon Kubler-Ross's (1953) five-stage framework. First, within the marriage, one or both of the partners deny the existence of problems and use this denial to maintain the relationship. When at least one of the partners confirms the stress and initiates the divorce, feelings of loss and depression occur. As the reality of the divorce becomes established, depression is replaced by anger, prominent in the stage of custody, access, and financial determination. The fourth stage, "reorientation of life-style and identity," involves a changing of habits and redirection of energy towards "the reworking of identity in all areas touched by marriage: personal, vocational, sexual and social." The final phase of acceptance occurs when "new patterns of interaction without the absent spouse have become firmly established" (Wiseman 1975:209-211). Kressel (1980) delineated four stages of divorce as part of a "general human adaptive mechanism": denial, mourning, anger, and readjustment. He saw this coping process as consisting of four major periods: a pre-divorce decision period, decision period, a period of negotiation, and a period of re-equilibration, noting a lack of recovery among the "non-initiators" as compared to the initiators of divorce.

However, neither formulation takes into account the unique loss of non-custodial fathers. The satisfactory resolution of the final stage of "acceptance," "reorientation of life-style and identity," or "readjustment" may be particularly problematic for fathers who are threatened with the loss of their children. In outlining their schema, neither Wiseman nor Kressel differentiate between women and men, those with or without children, or those with or without custody of their children. Because of their non-custodial status, the majority of fathers experience divorce in a radically different way than do other groups of divorced men and women:

> You get into a routine, a certain family way of life which you value deeply. It's impossible to adjust if this has meant a lot to you and you've suddenly lost it. I would have accepted the separation if it was just my wife and I—the fact that there's a child makes it impossible to accept. It's a total, complete upheaval—losing my son to me means having lost everything in life. It's like a life sentence, it's like prison (British "disengaged" father).

Particularly in their responses to open-ended questions regarding their children and the father-child relationship, the fathers in the study made frequent reference to their grief. Their responses reflect the fact that several years after the divorce, different fathers locate themselves at different stages of the bereavement continuum. A large number of fathers clearly had not reached the point of "acceptance" or "resolution"; many spoke of continuing depression and an overwhelming sense of loss, with themes of isolation, loneliness, and a total upheaval of their lives:

> I can only talk about my own experience, because each case is unique. It's very, very hard on me. I walk around in a perpetual cloud. It's ruined everything for me—screwed up my work, screwed up my personal life—it was everything; it was my whole existence. . . . it's left a kind of emptiness, a sadness. It's left a resignation... It's left a sort of cloud hanging on me. . . . I think an awful lot of people, when they meet me, think perhaps afterwards, "There's something about that person but I can't put my finger on it." But it's something tangible—because people have very strong reactions to it (Canadian "disengaged" father).

> I don't think I'll ever stop hurting—it's hurt me ever since the separation, and I think it'll hurt me for the rest of my life. The whole thing has just been such a waste, such a sad waste (British "disengaged" father).

The grief of non-custodial fathers is also reflected in a high incidence of physical and mental health problems subsequent to divorce. Fifty-five percent of fathers reported new physical health problems, while 61 percent described mental health difficulties they had not experienced prior to the divorce. Depression was mentioned by almost half the respondents, and a high proportion reported a number of depressive symptoms, such as sleeplessness, reduced energy, and poor appetite—all classical symptoms in bereavement and loss. Fathers were also asked if and to what extent the divorce had affected their work or career: 69 percent (fifty-five) reported serious negative repercussions; of these, twenty-three fathers cited health problems as contributing to their difficulties. These patterns did not differ between the Canadian and British subsamples.

Multiple Losses

The number of fathers in the sample who experienced new physical and mental health problems, along with serious repercussions on their work or career, illustrates the degree of personal trauma that divorce entailed for them. These results complement those of earlier studies showing men to be particularly debilitated by divorce.

Like all divorced family members, fathers face multiple losses upon divorce. Bohannan's (1970) six "stations" of divorce can be seen to represent six distinct types of loss that occur simultaneously for all divorcing parents: the *emotional divorce* is the process of mourning the loss of the marital relationship; the *co-parental divorce* involves the process of redefining the rights and duties of each parent, including custody, access, and financial support, and the dynamics of the parent-child relationship of both parents are different than they were prior to the divorce; the *legal divorce* is the process of legal dissolution of the marriage which establishes the right to remarry; the *economic divorce* is the process of dividing the joint property, when each spouse becomes a separate economic unit; the *community divorce* involves the severance of bonds and sources of support from social systems in the community and the establishment of new ones, recognizing the new identities of the former couple as two individual units; and the *psychic divorce* is the process of each spouse developing an autonomous self-identity, differentiating himself or herself from the marital relationship and coping with feelings of failure and desertion. These and other losses are particularly pronounced for fathers, who typically face the simultaneous loss of their children, spouse, and dwelling place:

> One thing that very few people are really able to appreciate is that whoever it is who does not have custody, whoever it is who moves out of the home—that you are out there, you are in your flat or your room or whatever—you are away from your children, and your wife, and they are in a family home, in their familiar surroundings, your wife has the children there, be they crutches, or be they a great joy, but they are people who care about each other, they are a threesome, and you are the isolated one. That can be absolute desolation, and you really can't

(whoever has the children can't) ever really, really even start to perceive how isolated one feels in the absence of your family. And that I think is perhaps the greatest tragedy of all. One may say verbally "that's really difficult," but if you face that for three or four years, it's really a very hard cross to bear (British "contact" father).

The inhibition of emotional expression, largely a product of men's socialization, inhibits the "working through" of these multiple losses for fathers. Many fathers, in describing their grief, talked of feeling compelled to disguise their symptoms and to present a "facade of coping" to the world. They were unlikely to seek or obtain any kind of support at the time of divorce: only twenty-eight of eighty fathers made use of any type of social support, whether informal (family or friends), semiformal (work and community contacts), or formal (agencies and professionals).

Grief and Child Absence

Both men and women experience multiple losses upon divorce. But, once again, for non-custodial fathers divorce presents a strain not comparable to that of mothers: the threatened or actual loss of their children. Of all potential adjustments, the most compelling problem for fathers is their pervasive sense of the loss of their children, and it is with the realization of this loss in particular that the classical symptoms of bereavement become manifest.

Such a formulation is a departure from the current emphasis in the literature on the loss of the marital relationship as being most salient for divorced men (in studies not controlling for the presence of children in the marriage or for custodial/non-custodial status), which effectively ignores fathers' attachment bonds with their children. Because the grief of fathers is directly and primarily linked to their experience of "child absence" above all other transitions faced during and after divorce, the most "at-risk" group of divorced men may be non-custodial fathers of dependent children.

Fathers' emotional investment in and attachment to their children is extremely strong. For fathers, divorce represents the threatened or actual loss of a primary attachment. When such attachment bonds are threatened, powerful attachment behaviour such as clinging, crying out, and angry coercion and protest are activated (Bowlby 1977), whereas a full grieving process is the "normal" reaction to an actual loss (Parkes and Weiss 1983). The degree of bereavement is dependent on the strength of the attachment to the lost person: the more intense the pre-existing relationship between the two, the more complex the mourning and the greater the probability of a poor outcome. Initial reactions of intense yearning (characteristic of those with previously intense attachments) are particularly strong predictors of poor outcome (Parkes and Weiss 1983).

Fathers were asked what they considered to be the most difficult aspects of their relationship with their children following the divorce (see Table 6). The great majority of non-custodial fathers (seventy-three of eighty) indicated some form of difficulty in the father-child relationship after divorce. No contact or not enough contact with their children was a prevailing theme for thirty-eight, and though only six fathers made direct reference to their depression (in this open-ended question), the majority of the remaining responses were infused with a sense of loss, sadness, or hopelessness in regard to some aspect of the father-child relationship during and/or after the divorce.

Table 6. Negative Aspects of the Post-Divorce Father-Child Relationship

Negative Aspects Identified	Times Mentioned
No contact	29
Loss of paternal influence in child's life	24
Not enough contact (time constraints of present relationship)	9
Child's unresolved feelings regarding the divorce/continuing negative effects of divorce on children	9
Discipline and behavioural problems of child	9
Lack of daily paternal care/routine	8
Separating from each other after visit	8
General concern for child's welfare and development	8
Father relegated to "visitor" status/ not "real father"	6
Father feels like "intruder" in child's life	6
Father's depression/sense of loss	6
No negative aspects	7

Maximum of four negative aspects per father.

In the period during divorce, with the sudden break in their pattern of contact with their children and the loss of familiarity in the father-child relationship, grief was a predominant reaction of the great majority of fathers in the sample. Subsequent to the period during divorce, however, there appeared to be significant differences in the course of "grief work" for fathers. While some remained "stuck" at some point along the bereavement continuum, others were able to successfully "work through" their grief and come to a level of acceptance of the loss. These differences were reflected in fathers' responses when asked about the positive aspects of their relationship with their children following the divorce (see Table 7).

Table 7.   Positive Aspects of the Post-Divorce Father-Child Relationship

Positive Aspects Identified	Times Mentioned
Closer bond/relationship	21
"Still a father"/continuing paternal influence in child's life	12
Continuing good bond/relationship	7
Luxury of having child to oneself/no interference from spouse	7

Maximum of two responses per father.

A large number of fathers replied that there were no positive aspects of their relationship with their children after the divorce. Other fathers, however, reported a closer bond or relationship with their children after divorce, with some indicating that they now in fact had more (or more "quality") time together. Clearly, the outcome for fathers is not universally bleak. For some divorce eventually led to positive outcomes for their relationships with their children.

Child Absence: Loss or Threatened Loss of Children

Fathers' descriptions of the grief they experienced during divorce in relation to the loss of the pre-divorce father-child relationship referred to one or more of the following: the threatened or actual loss of their children in the form of insufficient or no contact; the loss of the previous paternal role; and problems with the new "visiting" relationship. These interrelated factors constitute the three essential elements of the grief of non-custodial fathers during divorce.

Child absence is defined by legal custody and access determinations and the actual amount of contact between fathers and their children during and after divorce. Both de jure and de facto arrangements made during the initial stages of the divorce determine the level of father-child contact loss and fathers' perception of threatened loss. Here we follow Greif's (1979:312) definition of *child absence* as "a concept that pertains to reorganization of family structure as a result of a legal process (i.e., legal marital separation or divorce) and that eventuates in separation of parent and child." Parenting for non-custodial fathers is circumscribed by legal access awards and what the custodial parent will actually allow. Upon divorce, non-custodial fathers face an abrupt discontinuity in the form of their daily contact: access is usually circumscribed on a schedule not of the father's own choosing, and often according to what is considered to be a "customary" pattern of twice a month overnight or weekends (Wallerstein and Kelly 1980).

Fathers were asked how their children's absence affected them. Eighty-five percent (sixty-eight of eighty) of fathers primarily indicated some type of negative effect, 3 percent (two) positive, 6 percent (five) both positive and negative, and 6 percent (five) neither positive nor negative (or no effect) (see Table 8). Fathers' responses evidenced a full range of "grieflike" reactions to the absence of their children, with the majority indicating depression (50 percent) or depressive symptoms. Also frequently mentioned were feelings of isolation, guilt, anger, and constant worry—all representing different stages along the bereavement continuum.

Table 8.   Child Absence Effects

Negative Effects	Times Mentioned
Depression/sense of loss	40
Constant worry/yearning for children	27
Reference to loss of paternal influence/ loss of daily routine with children	17
Isolation/"emptiness"	14
Façade of coping	9
Guilt	9
Reference to loss of "family life"	8
Generally negative/"bad in every way"	8
Powerlessness/hopelessness of situation	7
Like death/dying	7

Maximum of three responses per father.

> I guess what's been taken away is my right to father my own son. It's like a constant stab in the heart. I feel anger and I feel hurt. My son has been stolen from me, as far as I am concerned, and there's no justification for it (Canadian "disengaged" father).

> Lousy. Simply a great sense of loss. I miss them like hell. There's been a lot of time spent dwelling on the way things might have been, thinking about them and what they might be doing, even what they might be doing together. There's a lot of sadness. It's affected me very strongly emotionally. My life has taken a completely different direction—not one which I would have chosen—and given the opportunity I certainly would choose to go back to my old life. I feel that having developed this relationship with the kids that was suddenly cut off—it's like losing part of my body (British "disengaged" father).

I try very hard not to think about it. It's very painful. There's just nothing I can do. I just feel helpless. I can't do anything to help them and I can't do anything toward being with them. I can't be a part of their lives, I can't teach them anything, I can't have any influence on them. I don't know—it's like a different world—I'm in one world and they're in another (Canadian "disengaged" father).

Just like a sort of hole in your life, a loss, as if someone's died (Canadian "contact" father).

Fathers were also asked for their perceptions of the effects of *father absence* on their children. Seventy-nine percent (sixty-three) primarily indicated some type of negative effect, 4 percent (three) positive, 4 percent (three) both positive and negative, 10 percent (eight) neither positive nor negative (or no effects), and 4 percent (three) stated that they did not know (see Table 9). The majority of fathers perceived a variety of negative effects of father absence, often believing that their children's physical and mental health and emotional well-being were seriously at risk without their father's regular involvement in their lives.

Table 9.   Father Absence Effects

Negative Effects	Times Mentioned
No father/male figure	20
On emotional development	17
Depression/misses father	16
Not having day-to-day (routine) input of father/ not being with or knowing father on daily basis	12
Confusion/instability/insecurity	9
Child exposed to unhealthy or negative environment/living arrangement	9
On social development/behavioural problems	8
Child's perception of divorce and father absence: self-blame	8
No sense of "family"/being "part of a family"	7
On personality development/moral development	7
Mother's/other adults' negative influence	7
On intellectual development/academic problems at school	6

Maximum of three responses per father.

Fathers were also asked (in relation to the period during divorce) how they had thought the divorce would affect their children. Sixty-eight percent (fifty-four) indicated having felt that it would effect them negatively, 5 percent (four) that it would have positive effects, 10 percent (eight) both positive and negative effects, 9 percent (seven) neither positive nor negative (or no) effects, and 9 percent (seven) stated that they did not know.

Perceived effects of both father absence and the divorce on children were significantly related to initiator of divorce. Fathers whose wives had initiated the divorce were much more likely to indicate negative effects of father absence ($p<.001$) and negative effects of divorce in general on their children ($p<.01$). These results corroborate those of Wallerstein and Kelly (1980:100): "How the parents saw their children during this post-separation period was often impossible to separate from their overriding need to justify their own role in the divorce." Fathers who initiated the divorce were more likely to perceive their children to be adjusting well and, conversely, those whose wives had been the initiators were more likely to regard their children as experiencing serious difficulty. However, the majority of fathers in both groups perceived the effects of father absence and the divorce to be negative.

> You have a sense of a tremendous unhappiness. You can see that they've been wounded. Well, when I saw them, their responses to me often depended on my ex-wife's responses to me—when my ex-wife was friendly to me, they'd be friendly; when my ex-wife was angry, all the anger that my kids felt about not having a father came to the surface and they didn't want to have anything to do with me. So their feelings towards me were really, really mixed. On the one hand sometimes they were warm to me, on the other hand they'd almost hate me. It was extremely hard to build up any relationship with them. They'd go through all kinds of phases—everything from being really clingy to me, very possessive, being afraid that I'd go away, to being cool and aloof. They had a sense of sadness about them, you could see it in their eyes, and they always seemed to have the need for the affection of a man, of a father—because they were always extremely close to me—always, especially my older daughter. As soon as I'd come home from work she'd always scream, whenever she was in the house, as soon as she heard the door open, she'd go, "Daddy!" and run the length of the house into my arms (Canadian "disengaged" father).

> They have to seek images elsewhere. They feel they have to be more self-sufficient; they get more self-reliant. But they also feel hurt and lack the pride of being loved—they feel emotionally deprived. It affects their self-image—they figure if you don't see them, you don't love them (Canadian "contact" father).

Role Loss

Related to the threatened or actual loss of one's children after divorce is the loss of a particular role or set of functions that together constitute the "father" role. The less a father's actual involvement with his child during divorce, the less his sense of having an ongoing parental role in the child's life. A clear danger of child absence, according to Greif (1979), is perceived role loss, leading to further withdrawal from the child. Child absence produces a significant change in a father's perception of his functioning as a parent, and this becomes self-reinforcing: fathers who see themselves as important in their fathering roles seek to continue these roles; fathers who do not perceive themselves as important in the fathering role are less motivated to maintain that role (Greif 1979).

> I would say that there has to be a distancing in the relationship. The closeness that previously existed would be eroded. And I think even more basic than that, the children wouldn't really regard the father as being a father in the sense of that role—certainly not as somebody as important in their lives as their mother—which previously would have been the case. When you're living as a family, each parent is equally important, maybe in different ways, but equally important, in the lives of the children. Once you've left, the only person who's important in their lives is the mother. The father isn't there and is somebody that they go to from time to time. That becomes a relationship they can live without (British "disengaged" father).

Greif (1979) measured fathers' perceptions of changes in the fathering role subsequent to divorce, and her classification of ten general roles that fathers perform in relation to their children is replicated here. Chapter 2 reported fathers' perception of the degree of their influence in these areas before the divorce. They were then asked for their present (post-divorce) level of influence with respect to each of the roles (see Tables 10 and 11).

Table 11.   Perceived Change in Paternal Influence on Children (before and after Divorce)

Paternal Roles	Increase %(N)	No Change %(N)	Decrease %(N)	Total %(N)
Routine daily care and safety	6(5)	5(4)	89(71)	100(80)
Intellectual development	8(6)	19(15)	74(59)	100(80)
Teaching behaviour/ social skills	3(2)	21(17)	76(61)	100(80)
Personality development	6(5)	21(17)	73(58)	100(80)
Emotional development	10(8)	18(14)	73(58)	100(80)
Giving child(ren) a feeling of being part of a family	11(9)	16(13)	73(58)	100(80)
Physical development	5(4)	28(22)	68(54)	100(80)
Financial affairs of children	6(5)	28(22)	66(53)	100(80)
Moral development	13(10)	28(22)	60(48)	100(80)
Religious development	6(5)	44(35)	50(40)	100(80)

Paternal roles are listed in order of amount of decrease in influence.

Greif's study (which included a number of joint custody fathers in a sample of forty middle-class fathers who all had some level of post-divorce contact with their children) concluded that divorced fathers as a group do not perceive a change in paternal influence after divorce, with the exception of a significant decrease in "making children feel part of a family." The present study, more representative of the non-custodial father population insofar as half the sample was comprised of "disengaged" fathers (equal to the proportion in the general population), with the remaining fathers having a range of levels of contact with their children, produced quite different results: in all ten areas of parental functioning, non-custodial fathers as a group ranked their influence on their children as significantly lower after the divorce compared to their pre-divorce level. Of particular interest is the fact that the most marked decrease was in the area of the routine daily care and safety of children.

Fathers were also asked about their perceptions of their parenting abilities now, after the divorce, as compared to during the marriage. Though fathers reported a marked loss of influence in all major areas of their children's lives and in their actual role as parents, they also generally felt that, in spite of this, their parenting abilities had remained intact and, given the opportunity, they would again be able to function as effective parents.

Table 10. Perceived Paternal Influence on Children After Divorce

Paternal Roles	Very High/High %(N)	Medium %(N)	Low/very Low %(N)	No Influence %(N)	Total %(N)
Routine daily care and safety	3(2)	18(14)	31(25)	49(39)	100(80)
Intellectual development	13(10)	14(11)	31(25)	43(34)	100(80)
Physical development	19(15)	13(10)	25(20)	44(35)	100(80)
Personality development	16(13)	14(11)	29(23)	41(33)	100(80)
Teaching Behaviou/social skills	15(12)	15(12)	29(23)	41(33)	100(80)
Emotional development	15(12)	18(14)	25(20)	43(34)	100(80)
Religious development	14(11)	8(6)	30(24)	49(39)	100(80)
Moral development	26(21)	10(8)	20(16)	44(35)	100(80)
Giving child(ren) a feeling of being part of a family	26(21)	5(4)	23(18)	46(37)	100(80)
Financial affairs of child(ren)	16(13)	19(15)	25(20)	40(32)	100(80)

The "Visiting" Relationship

For non-custodial fathers, the development of a new type of parental identity is crucial in reaching an acceptance of the loss of the pre-divorce father-child relationship and a resolution of the grieving process. It is through established access arrangements that the non-custodial father can develop this new identity.

The redefinition of one's role as a parent has been identified as one of the most difficult tasks of the non-custodial parent. The non-custodial parent-child "visiting" relationship:

> has no counterpart, and therefore no model, within the intact family. Its parameters, its limits, and its potentialities are new and remain to be explored.... The parent who moves out of the household begins a new role for which there is no dress rehearsal and no script. A visiting relationship between parent and child is strange by its very nature (Wallerstein and Kelly 1980:121-123).

Little formal assistance is available to non-custodial fathers to help them learn what this new role entails and how they might exercise it in the best interests of their children: where to meet, how often to visit, how long to visit, the number of children to visit at one time, and what to do during the visit. Fathers are also faced with how to relate to their children: what to talk about, what to share of their own lives, how to exercise discipline and manage their children's behaviour, and how to deal with the various emotions surrounding the visit. Fathers must restructure their previous relationship with their children along unfamiliar dimensions: the post-divorce father-child relationship is structured by the arranged patterns and constraints of the "visits" and this structure sets the limits for the new relationship (Wallerstein and Kelly 1980).

Fathers were asked how the new "visiting" relationship had affected them. Eighty-four percent (sixty-seven of eighty) primarily indicated some type of negative effect, 9 percent (seven) positive, 3 percent (two) both positive and negative, and 5 percent (four) neither positive nor negative (or no effect) (see Table 12).

Table 12.   "Visiting" Effects on Fathers

Negative Effects	Times Mentioned
Feel like "visitor" or "uncle" in child's life/not "real father"	29
Depression/sadness/sense of loss	26
Artificial, unnatural, strained nature of visits	17
Difficulty separating from child after visits	16
No influence in child's life	15
Generally painful to visit	15
Constant worry/guilt when child not present	9
Loneliness/miss day-to-day contact and routine	9

Maximum of three responses per father.

Fathers identified a variety of constraints in "visiting," with the greatest number describing the avuncular nature of the relationship and the fact that "visiting" in no way constituted "real fatherhood."

> I think it's devastating on the father because if the father is a truly loving person he wants to care and be part of the nurturing of the children, and just visiting is not doing that. Fathers need to know that they can provide a home for the children. Just going out and visiting, the father is not performing a fathering role—it's more like a friend role. And children need more than a friend in a father (Canadian "disengaged" father).

> There's a tremendous feeling of frustration, a great sense of loss in contributing really very little to the lives of the kids. Missing the stages of growing up. All sorts of day-to-day things which are part of normal family life—being familiar with the kids' progress in school, their friends, their interests, even things like what they like to eat. All these little things sort of build up into the blocks which form a relationship, and suddenly all those blocks are removed. And it gives you very little on which to really build a relationship (British "disengaged" father).

Most spoke of their dissatisfaction with becoming mere "visitors" in their children's lives. Several referred to the pain of the visits themselves, and the artificial and strained atmosphere surrounding the visits. Without a day-to-day familiarity, fathers and children experienced an awkwardness at the start of each visit; saying "goodbye" was a particularly painful reminder of the loss of living with each other on a full-time basis:

I'm crushed when I have to take him home. A weekend isn't enough. I feel like I'm abandoning him when I have to take him back—it's like I feel I'm constantly wounding him each time. But I'm not abandoning him by choice, it's because I have to (Canadian "disengaged" father).

It had a devastating effect on me. I had to readjust to the fact that I really did have two sons, but who were not close to me any more. When they came we were able to get close, but the heartache would really begin when they had to leave. I mean, that feeling has never ever left me. Everytime I had to say "Cheerio" to those boys, they were in agony, their hearts are in turmoil, and so is mine. I just find it all so sad—it's total agony and turmoil (British "disengaged" father).

It's heartbreaking, actually. It's very different to go and see them and then walk away, and to know that you can't put them to bed at night, see them get up in the morning and go away to school, to see Susan starting school next year for the first time, you're not going to see her in her school uniform for the first day of school, and now Christmas is coming up, which is going to be a very bad time for me, it's going to be really difficult. In simple terms, it just cracks you up. Just visiting them is like reliving the separation over and over. I know often I feel I don't want to see them at all—but I know I do (British "disengaged" father).

Fathers were also asked how they perceived the "visiting" relationship to have affected their children (se Table 13). Sixty-four percent (fifty-one) of fathers primarily indicated some type of negative effect, 10 percent (eight) positive, 15 percent (twelve) both positive and negative, and 6 percent (five) neither positive nor negative (or no effect). Four percent (three) of fathers stated that "visiting" effects depended on the nature of the post-divorce relationship between the parents, and one father indicated that he was not aware of the effects because he had no contact with his children.

Table 13. "Visiting" Effects on Children

Negative Effects	Times Mentioned
Depression/sadness/misses father	17
Difficulty separating from father after visits	17
Generally painful to visit	17
Artificial, unnatural, strained nature of visits	15
Confusion/instability/insecurity	13
Disengagement or emotional withdrawal of child from father/father seen as "intruder" into child's routine	10
Child overindulged during visits	10
Distorted perception of "father"/perception of father as "uncle", "brother", "friend" or "visitor"	6
Behavioural and discipline problems/"lack of respect" of father	6

Maximum of three responses per father.

Although the majority of fathers reported primarily negative effects of "visiting" on their children, more fathers reported positive effects on their children than on themselves. They also reported higher levels of negative effects of father absence on their children than of "visiting." The "father absence" element was identified as one of the most problematic aspects of the "visiting" relationship for children. In general, fathers tended to ascribe the effects of "visiting" on their children as similar to the effects on themselves: sadness, depression, and a sense of loss; difficulty separating after visits; the pain of the visits; and the artificial, unnatural, and strained nature of the visits.

> I think it's highlighted when I have to return them: the child screaming on the doorstep, and it's tearing your heart out, and all you can do is to give him a hug and a kiss and say, "Goodbye, be a good kid, I'll see you soon." I really think it's never enough (Canadian "contact" father).

Fathers' desire for their children not to be hurt or unhappy, feelings of guilt, and fear of children's disapproval, anger, or rejection, often led to fathers playing the stereotypical "Santa Claus" role (which they themselves perceived to be highly unsatisfactory), with visits that involved entertainment and gifts, and fathers being generally unwilling or unable to discipline their children:

I think it affects them greatly—it's torture on them. I've seen so many times when a father has to bring his son back, and his son doesn't want to go back. The father has such a short time with his child, he spoils him rotten—because the environment has made him that way. If the father was with the child on a day-to-day basis, the child wouldn't be so spoiled and overindulged, and unhappy all the time about having to leave his father, and not being with his father. . . . In the long term, a child can grow up to hate the mother, or the custodial father. And the reason I say that is that everytime the child gets a weekend with dad, dad spoils him, whereas he goes back to mom, and mom makes him do his homework, clean his room—and dad doesn't. So as he grows up, the child develops a picture in his mind which says, "Dad's the good guy, mom's the bad guy" (Canadian "disengaged" father).

In sum, the most salient characteristic of the divorce experience of non-custodial fathers in general is the fact that the great majority of fathers—as a consequence of the absence of their children, loss of their previous parental role, and the constraints of the new "visiting" relationship—experience a bereavement of sufficient strength to produce new physical and mental health problems. There were no differences between the Canadian and British subgroups in this regard. The intensity and course of the grieving process of non-custodial fathers was equivalent in both locales.

4

Discontinuity Between Pre-Divorce and Post-Divorce Father-Child Relationships

Though the majority of all non-custodial fathers manifest a grief reaction in the initial period during divorce, with the passage of time clear differences begin to emerge among fathers. While many fathers continue, well after the divorce, to display symptoms associated with bereavement and portray themselves as being "stuck" in the grieving process, many others are able to successfully work through initial difficulties and eventually develop meaningful attachments with their children within the confines of the "visiting" relationship. The fathers who appeared to arrive at some level of resolution of their grief and to make a positive transition to divorce were those who were able to maintain regular contact with their children. There *are* positive outcomes of divorce for many non-custodial fathers. Several of those who had ongoing contact with their children described the divorce as helping them to actually expand their involvement with their children.

The positive outcomes of divorce for the father-child relationship, however, are largely overshadowed by the predominantly negative effects described earlier. Non-custodial fathers have a strong likelihood of becoming disengaged fathers. As noted earlier, in 52 percent of Furstenberg's (1983) sample of 1,337 children of divorce, the last contact between fathers and their children had been one or more years prior, only one-third of the children averaged monthly or more contact with their fathers, and more than twice as many had no contact with their father in the past 5 years as had visited with him once a week or more—36 percent versus 16 percent.

Link between Pre- and Post-Divorce Father-Child Relationships

The issue of non-custodial fathers' contact with and/or disengagement from their children has not been empirically or systematically examined, but it is commonly assumed that post-divorce father-child relationships will largely reflect those previously existing within the marriage. That is, those fathers assuming a comparatively active role with their children before the divorce will want to maintain and will strive to continue such involvement after divorce and hence are the group most likely to have ongoing (post-divorce) contact. These fathers, because of their involvement with their children, are more likely to form strong attachment bonds that they will actively seek to preserve. Conversely, it is expected that those fathers who locate themselves on the periphery of their children's lives before the divorce will be the group most likely to lose contact; they will become the "disengaged" fathers.

The assumption that the father-child relationship will be broadly continuous in the post-divorce period with that which had obtained during the marriage is in accord with prevailing "common sense" notions and with psychological theory. Wallerstein and Kelly (1980), however, in looking at the patterns of contact between non-custodial fathers and their children, discovered that the relation between pre- and post-divorce patterns was surprisingly varied. They found that the way in which a non-custodial father managed to define his post-divorce parenting role was not always correlated with the nature of his pre-divorce role. Eighteen months after divorce (separation), there was no correlation between the visiting patterns that had emerged and the pre-divorce father-child relationship. Contrary to "common sense" formulations, they found no differences between those non-custodial fathers who had remained in contact and those who had disengaged from their children's lives in the level of their involvement with and attachment to their children before the divorce. In a five-year follow-up, the authors continued to find no correlation between the closeness in father-child relationships before and after divorce: 25 percent of the fathers in their study grew more distant from their children in the space of five years, but another 25 percent actually grew closer (Wallerstein and Kelly 1980).

Our sample of non-custodial fathers may be more representative of the general population of such fathers than that of Wallerstein and Kelly (1980), who drew their sample from a clinical population of parents and their children and provided a counselling service aimed partly at ensuring ongoing contact between fathers and their children. In comparing the two subgroups of contact and disengaged fathers, one of the objectives of our study was to examine whether pre- and post-divorce father-child relationship patterns were similar to those identified by Wallerstein and Kelly, or whether they tended to conform to the "common sense" formulation. In fact, the results of this study differed from those of Wallerstein and Kelly (1980), yet diverged even further from what "common sense" notions would assume. A more striking discontinuity between pre- and post-divorce father-child relationships was observed in our study: rather than there being no correlation between pre- and post-divorce patterns, there appeared to be a strong *inverse* relationship. Fathers who described themselves as having been highly involved with and attached to their children, influential in their development, and sharing "family work" tasks before the divorce were more likely to have *lost* contact with their children after divorce than fathers who had defined themselves in a more traditional manner, being peripherally involved and reporting lower levels of father-child attachment. The fathers scoring lowest on indices of infant and child care, attachment to their children, influence in various areas of their child's development, and on measures of androgyny before the divorce, were more likely to *remain* in contact with their children after divorce.

Discontinuity between Pre- and Post-Divorce Father-Child Relationships

In relation to most indices of infant and child care, emotional attachment, and perceived level of influence in various areas of children's growth and development, marked differences emerged between the contact and disengaged fathers in the study. While the majority of disengaged fathers viewed the divorce as severing what had been close affective bonds between their children and themselves, most of the contact fathers described themselves as having been less directly involved and attached and often did not see the divorce as significantly diminishing the relationship.

Problems do arise over the validity of this finding; the self-report and retrospective nature of the study remains an important limitation. It may be argued that disengaged fathers' high reported levels of pre-divorce involvement with, attachment to, and influence on their children is largely an artifact of recall: the importance of interaction with one's children may be heightened by separation from them, and disengaged fathers in particular may tend to embellish the former relationship. Corroborative data from other members of the divorced family is not available, and access to information about the former father-child relationship was not obtainable, other than that given solely by the fathers themselves by their recollection.

However, overall reported rates of pre-divorce paternal involvement, attachment, and influence (from the entire sample of contact and disengaged fathers) were observed to fall within the reported range of paternal participation in the two-parent family in existing studies of the father role. Specifically, Kamo (1988) found that, on the average, husbands carry 36 percent of the total domestic workload (domestic tasks plus child care), which increases to 41 percent when both spouses are employed full-time and 43 percent when both earn approximately the same amount of money; Martin and Roberts (1984) found that although 44 percent of married women in Britain working full-time said they shared overall family work (domestic tasks plus child care), 67 percent saw child care as shared. The overall mean levels of paternal participation reported here, in a range of infant care tasks, for example (ranging from 24 percent to 46 percent, relative to their wives' involvement), are well within the range of these and other studies (40 percent in Warner [1986]; and 27 percent in Berk [1985]). Thus the aggregate rates of the pre-divorce levels of paternal involvement, attachment, and influence of this sample of fathers (contact and disengaged) largely correspond to the aggregate levels found in other studies of male parenting.

Further, fathers' involvement with and attachment to their children before the divorce were measured by means of a number of discrete indices; multiple measures relevant to the same dimension were used. Questions gauging fathers' involvement in specific tasks were included in an effort to minimize the effects of retrospection, and, on each of these, disengaged fathers consistently reported significantly higher levels of involvement than contact fathers. Several questions relating to attitudes and ideologies regarding gender roles in the family were checked against fathers' self-ratings on those indices, and fathers' reported ideologies were observed to closely correspond to their reported rates of involvement with, attachment to, and influence on their children. Finally, on all questions of an open-ended nature, disengaged fathers demonstrated as vivid a recall of pre-divorce patterns and events as contact fathers, with many examples and illustrations of their pre-divorce bond. Disengaged fathers were particularly conscious of the negative impact of various aspects of the divorce process on their children, a reflection of their previous attachment. At the very least, it is significant that disengaged fathers especially stressed the value and importance of active and affective fathering in their children's growth and development, and the damaging consequences of the loss of the father-child relationship on their children's adjustment to divorce.

Observed Differences

In regard to their level of involvement (relative to their wives' contribution) in a variety of infant care tasks, significant differences were observed between contact and disengaged fathers in reported rates of playing with the baby, lulling the baby to sleep, and taking the baby for a walk, with disengaged fathers reporting higher rates of participation (all $p<.01$), as well as in taking the baby to the doctor and looking after the baby when he or she was ill ($p<.05$). Slightly higher levels were also reported by disengaged fathers in bathing the baby, feeding the baby, and preparing the baby's meals ($p<.10$). In the realm of domestic tasks, there were fewer differences between the two groups, although disengaged fathers reported higher rates of involvement in doing the laundry ($p<.01$), household cleaning, and preparation of family meals (both $p<.05$).

There were also significant differences in the reported amount of contact fathers had with their children in the year before the divorce ($p<.05$). Contact fathers spent an average of twelve hours per week with their children alone and sixteen hours with others present, but disengaged fathers spent twenty hours alone and twenty hours with others.

In addition to fathers' reports of their actual behaviour within the marriage, their level of emotional attachment to their children was measured. As noted, non-custodial fathers in general reported a high level of emotional attachment to their children during the marriage. Here, too, however, significant differences emerged between the contact and disengaged subgroups. Disengaged fathers reported "very strong" attachment to their children to a significantly greater degree than contact fathers (p<.05), who more frequently reported "strong" and "moderate" attachment. This pattern was reflected in fathers' self-ratings on a number of attachment indices (thinking about children, wanting to be with children when not with them, comforting children when in distress, and discussing feelings with children). Disengaged fathers reported significantly higher levels (p<.01).

Also significant was the fact that almost all (thirty-eight of forty) disengaged fathers found their family role to be the most satisfying during the marriage, whereas only just over half (twenty-two of forty) of contact fathers did so, with eighteen of forty contact fathers indicating a primary attachment to their work or other non-family roles (p<.001).

Finally, in nine of the ten areas examined, disengaged fathers reported significantly higher levels of influence on their children's growth and development before the divorce than contact fathers. Differences between the two groups emerged in the routine daily care and safety of children, personality development, intellectual development, physical development, and moral development (all p<.01); and in giving children a feeling of being part of a family, teaching behaviour and social skills, emotional development, and religious development (all p<.05). The two groups had no significant differences in their pre-divorce influence on the financial affairs of their children.

Fathers' ideologies regarding gender role division within the family were also examined. If ideologies match reported levels of pre-divorce behavioural involvement, attachment, and influence, one may be more confident in asserting that the differences between contact and disengaged fathers are genuine. Quantitative and qualitative analysis revealed marked differences between contact and disengaged fathers in attitudes towards gender-role division in the family, fathers' reported strengths and weaknesses as parents during the marriage, and definitions of "fathering," "mothering," and "family life." Whereas contact fathers' responses were divided between "traditional" and "androgynous" orientations towards gender roles and division of labour within the family, the great majority of disengaged fathers tended towards an "androgynous" stance and expressed sentiments favouring an egalitarian division of family work.

When asked directly about gender-role division within the family ("Is there a fundamental difference in roles between the father and the mother in the family?"), clear differences emerged between contact and disengaged fathers (see Table 14).

**Table 14.   Paternal Contact by Fathers' Ideologies
Regarding Gender Roles**

Role Division within the Family	Contact %(N)	Disengaged %(N)	Total % (N)
No difference between "father" and "mother" role in family ("androgynous" orientation)	50(20)	82(33)	66(53)
Same difference between "father" and "mother" role in family ("mixed" orientation)	8(3)	8(3)	8(6)
Fundamental difference between "father" and "mother" role in family ("traditional" orientation)	42(17)	10(4)	26(21)
Total	100(40)	100(40)	100(80)

p<.01

In addition, significant differences between the contact and disengaged subgroups emerged when asked for their *definitions* of "fathering" and "mothering," with disengaged fathers more likely to equate the two (p<.01).

Rather than post-divorce patterns reflecting pre-divorce father-child relationships or there being no correlation between the two, there appears to be a strong inverse relationship, with significant differences consistently reported between contact and disengaged fathers in their pre-divorce involvement with, attachment to, and influence on their children, as well as in their attitudes and ideologies related to gender roles in the family. This pattern of discontinuity was equally evident in the Canadian and British subsamples.

Contact and Disengaged Fathers Compared

Demographically, there were no observable differences between contact and disengaged fathers. It was found, however, that differences emerged between the two groups in regard to a number of external factors, such as fathers' experiences with the legal system and their relationships with their former wives, and to internal factors, including fathers' experiences of the bereavement process and their reactions to child absence, role loss, and the constraints of the "visiting" relationship.

There were no apparent differences between contact and disengaged fathers in relation to age, length of marriage, length of separation, or occupation and income of respondent. The sex and age of the children involved were marginal in determining whether a father continued ongoing contact or became disengaged. The initiator of separation also was not a statistically significant factor with respect to contact and disengagement, although in thirty of the fifty-four wife-initiated divorces, fathers subsequently lost contact, whereas in sixteen of the twenty-six husband- or mutually initiated divorces they remained involved. Whether or not a father was legally divorced was not associated with post-divorce paternal contact, nor was remarriage of the father (this lack of an association is qualified by the fact that only nine of the eighty fathers in our study had remarried; of these, three were disengaged fathers).

Surprisingly, paternal contact did not seem to be associated with various "practical" difficulties identified in the literature as potentially inhibiting a divorced father's subsequent contact with his children. Post-divorce paternal contact was not associated with either the type and size of the father's accommodation after divorce or the distance between the father's residence and that of his children. Adequate accommodation and close proximity did not ensure paternal contact. The majority of *both* contact and disengaged fathers did not consider distance, transportation, finances, or work schedule as significant problems in relation to contact with their children.

Legal and Other External Factors

An important component of non-custodial fathers' experiences during and after divorce was their contact with lawyers and the legal system. Seventy-five of the fathers had at least consulted a lawyer. A number of important differences emerged between contact and disengaged fathers in terms of the legal aspects of the divorce.

There was no significant difference between contact and disengaged fathers in their pattern of contesting custody: of the fifteen non-custodial fathers who had contested the issue of maternal custody in court, nine remained in contact with their children and six became disengaged. There was no relationship between paternal contact and spousal disagreement over the issue of custody at the time of the divorce, nor was there any difference between the two groups in terms of desired legal custody outcome. There was a difference, however, in relation to desired *physical* custody of the children at the time of the divorce ($p<.05$): disengaged fathers expressed a desire for at least partial physical custody with greater frequency than contact fathers. Also, when asked about their desired level of contact with their children after divorce, disengaged fathers expressed a desire for increased levels with much greater frequency than contact fathers ($p<.001$). Thus from the point of divorce, at which time they report a greater desire for at least partial physical custody, disengaged fathers' requirements for post-divorce contact with their children appear to be greater than those of contact fathers.

The frequency of legal determinations of maternal custody in the sample did not vary significantly between contact and disengaged fathers, although in ten of the fifteen cases where maternal custody arrangements had not been legally ratified, fathers remained in contact with their children. There was no relationship between paternal contact and the mode of legal custody determination (mutually between father and mother, negotiated via lawyers, or court action), although in three of the four mutually-arranged determinations, fathers remained in contact with their children.

There were significant differences, however, between contact and disengaged fathers in their satisfaction with the legal maternal custody arrangement. Sixty-five fathers reported legal maternal custody determinations: twelve of the fourteen fathers satisfied with this legal arrangement were contact fathers, and thirty-three of the fifty-one dissatisfied were disengaged (p<.01). There were also differences in relation to fathers' reasons for dissatisfaction with the legal maternal custody arrangement, with legal custody determinations often cited by disengaged fathers as responsible for their loss of contact with their children (see Table 15).

Table 15. Paternal Contact by Reasons for Dissatisfaction with Legal Custody Arrangement

Reason	Contact %(N)	Disengaged %(N)	Total % (N)
Wanted paternal or joint custody	28(5)	27(9)	28(14)
Sole maternal custody seen to result in *no* paternal contact with children	–	27(9)	18(9)
Sole maternal custody seen to allow ex-wife to cut off contact between father and children	6(1)	24(8)	18(9)
Sole custody seen as not in children's best interests/welfare of children compromised	22(4)	12(4)	16(8)
Sole maternal custody seen to result in *not enough* paternal contact with children	33(6)	3(1)	14(7)
Father is left with no legal rights vis-à-vis children	11(2)	6(2)	8(4)
Total	100(18)	100(33)	100(51)

Maximum of two reasons recorded per respondent; the relative frequency of fathers' first reason are presented.
p<.01

In relation to legal access arrangements, there was no relationship between paternal contact and spousal disagreement over the issue of access at the time of the divorce, nor were there any differences between contact and disengaged fathers in whether or not there had been a legal determination of access, or the mode of legal access determination (mutually between father and mother, negotiation via lawyers, or court action). There were, however, clear differences between the two groups in the type of legal access arrangement that had been made: of the fifty-eight legal access arrangements made, all ten of the "reasonable access" determinations (seven of which were made in Canada) were associated with subsequent paternal disengagement (see Table 16).

Table 16.   Paternal Contact by Legal Access Arrangement

Type of Arrangement	Contact %(N)	Disengaged %(N)	Total % (N)
"Reasonable"	–	17(10)	17(10)
"Flexible"	2(1)	2(1)	3(2)
Defined	47(27)	29(17)	76(44)
Other/don't know	-	3(2)	3(2)
Total	48(28)	52(30)	100(58)

"Defined" access refers to arrangements wherein the exact parameters of paternal contact are specified.
p <.01

Where no legal access determinations were made, the frequency of paternal contact and disengagement was about equal. No legal determination, however, is not tantamount to a legal access determination without any clear guidelines: each case of "reasonable access" was followed by fathers' disengagement. Further, a determination of "holiday" or "vacation access" (one of the eleven defined access arrangements) was also associated with paternal disengagement— all five such determinations were followed by fathers' loss of contact with their children. If access is to be granted through the judicial system, specification of its exact parameters is much more likely to bode well for a father's continued contact with his children.

Not surprisingly, as with legal custody, significant differences between contact and disengaged fathers were reported in their satisfaction with the legal access arrangement. Fifty-eight fathers had had legal access determinations: all ten of the fathers satisfied with the arrangement were contact fathers, and twenty-nine of the forty-seven dissatisfied were disengaged from their children (p<.001).[4]

There were also differences between the two groups in relation to their reasons for dissatisfaction with the legal access arrangement (see Table 17).

Table 17. Paternal Custody by Reasons for Dissatisfaction with Legal Access Arrangement

Reason	Contact %(N)	Disengaged %(N)	Total % (N)
Too little access (or no residential access)	67(12)	14(4)	34(16)
Legal access arrangement seen to result in no paternal contact with children	–	52(15)	32(15)
Legal access arrangement seen to allow ex-wife to cut off contact between father and children	6(1)	17(5)	13(6)
Wanted paternal or joint custody	6(1)	10(3)	9(4)
Access arrangements seen as too rigid, constrained	6(1)	3(1)	4(2)
Other	18(3)	3(1)	9(4)
Total	100(18)	100(29)	100(47)

Maximum of two reasons recorded per respondent; the relative frequencies of fathers' first reason are presented.
p <.001

In contrast to the strong differences that emerged between contact and disengaged fathers in relation to their satisfaction with legal custody and access arrangements, there were no differences between the two groups in regard to their satisfaction with legal post-divorce financial arrangements (property settlement and support payments) or in regard to any aspects of the legal financial arrangement.

Interestingly, in relation to custody and access, there was no association between paternal contact and the type of advice fathers received from their lawyers. Further, there were no differences between contact and disengaged fathers in the nature of their lawyers' advice regarding legal custody and access. Fathers' overall ratings of lawyers in helping or hindering their subsequent relationship with their children, and of the judicial system in relation to its appropriateness as a forum for determining child custody and access arrangements, however, differed significantly between the two groups. Those fathers reporting that lawyers had helped, both helped and hindered, or had no effect on the subsequent father-child relationship were more likely to be contact fathers (eighteen of twenty-three fathers), while a greater proportion of the disengaged fathers stated that their lawyers had in some way hindered the relationship (thirty-one of fifty-two; p<.05). Although the great majority of both contact and disengaged fathers perceived the judicial system to be an inappropriate forum for determining child custody and access, all six of the fathers considering judicial resolution to be appropriate were contact fathers. A higher percentage of contact fathers reported satisfaction with the fairness of the court hearing regarding custody and/or access, while a higher proportion of disengaged fathers reported dissatisfaction (p<.05).

In sum, many important differences were found between contact and disengaged fathers in their experiences with lawyers and the judicial system. Disengaged fathers reported higher levels of overall dissatisfaction and more profound repercussions of the legal system on their subsequent relationship with their children. It appears, however, that because the nature of the actual advice given by lawyers on child custody and access (specifically their discouragement of custody and encouragement of access in most cases) did not differ between contact and disengaged fathers, the differences between the two groups in their experiences with lawyers and the legal system cannot be attributed to the differential behaviour of lawyers. Indeed, the *uniformity* of approach among lawyers and the largely unvarying nature of judicial resolution vis-à-vis custody and access towards a group with very different experiences of fatherhood before the divorce—thus applying a homogeneous approach to a heterogeneous population—may have contributed to disengaged fathers' high level of dissatisfaction and negative experiences. Contact and disengaged fathers enter the legal system with radically different family life experiences, with "now disengaged" fathers reporting consistently higher levels of pre-divorce involvement with, attachment to, and influence on their children, and "now contact" fathers defining themselves in a more traditional manner and more likely to have been on the periphery of their children's lives. Fathers with quantitatively and qualitatively different pre-divorce patterns and relationships with their children are subject to a system that does not differentiate between these patterns; this, it would seem, primarily accounts for the marked differences between contact and disengaged fathers in their reported experience with lawyers and the legal system.

Fathers were also asked about their experiences with other sources of help, both formal and informal, used at the time of the divorce. There were no apparent differences between contact and disengaged fathers in the frequency of use of other sources, the type of sources used, the kind of help or advice that was offered, and the effects of the help or advice offered and their subsequent relationships with their children.

One of the major repercussions of a judicial mode of determining post-divorce custody and access arrangements, according to both contact and disengaged fathers, is that the prevailing "adversarial" approach of lawyers and the legal system enhances or creates an oppositional atmosphere between the former spouses. Quite revealing in this context was the fact that while *no* differences emerged between contact and disengaged fathers in the level of conflict between the parents *at the time of the divorce(separation)*, there was a strong relationship between paternal contact and *post-divorce* conflict between the parents. That is, there were no differences between contact and disengaged fathers as to whether a calm or turbulent atmosphere existed at the time of the divorce (before any major legal involvement of the parties); the differences between the two groups emerged only after legal processes had had their impact. Thirty-nine of forty disengaged fathers assessed their post-divorce relationship with their former spouses as "unfriendly" or "non-existent," but only fourteen of the forty contact fathers did so; twenty-six of the contact fathers described the post-divorce contact between the ex-spouses concerning their children as "friendly" or "middling" (p<.001).

For the great majority (thirty-four of forty) of disengaged fathers, contact with their ex-wives was reported as "non-existent." For non-custodial fathers, discontinued contact with the former spouse clearly does not bode well for continued contact with one's children: only six fathers had managed to remain in contact with their children despite the loss of contact with their former spouse.

Paternal contact was strongly related to former wives' encouragement or discouragement of fathers' contact with their children after divorce, with *all* forty disengaged fathers indicating that their ex-wives had actively discouraged contact, compared with only fourteen contact fathers (p<.001). For the majority of fathers, some level of encouragement on the part of their former spouses was necessary to facilitate ongoing contact with their children, although fourteen of forty fathers were able to remain in contact despite their ex-wives' discouragement. There were also differences between contact and disengaged fathers in the *ways* their former spouses had discouraged post-divorce father-child contact, with outright refusal of access being much more predominant among disengaged fathers (see Table 18).

Table 18.   Paternal Contact by Mothers' Discouragment of Father-Child Contact after Divorce

Methods of Discouragement	Contact %(N)	Disengaged %(N)	Total % (N)
Refusal of access	19(3)	45(18)	38(21)
Criticism of father to children	6(1)	15(6)	13(7)
Periodic refusal of access/refusal of residential access	25(4)	5(2)	11(6)
Children not ready for access visit/arrangements changed at "last minute"	6(1)	10(4)	9(5)
Moving with children to unknown location	–	10(4)	7(4)
Legal action	19(3)	3(1)	7(4)
Confrontation at time of access visit	-	8(3)	5(3)
Using children as "pawns" or "go-betweens"	13(2)	–	4(2)
Refusal of telephone contact	–	3(1)	2(1)
Using access as lever to obtain financial concessions	6(1)	–	2(1)
Putting onus on father to arrange access	6(1)	–	2(1)
Punishing child for visiting	–	3(1)	2(1)
Total	100(16)[5]	100(40)	100(56)[6]

Maximum of three per respondent; the relative frequencies of the first method cited by fathers are presented.
p<.01

In sum, marked differences exist between contact and disengaged fathers not only in regard to their experiences with lawyers and the judicial system, but also in their post-divorce relationship patterns with their former spouses. These two related factors are critical in determining the *consequences* of divorce for fathers; that is, the actual boundaries of the post-divorce father-child relationship.

Grief Reaction and Other Internal Factors

Fathers' *adjustment* to the consequences of divorce similarly influence the nature of post-divorce father-child relationships. The process of grieving took a radically different course for contact and disengaged fathers. Contact fathers were able to establish new relationships with their children within the confines of the "visiting" relationship in the critical period during divorce and arrived at a level of resolution of their grief, but disengaged fathers were largely unsuccessful in this regard.

The grief of non-custodial fathers is reflected in the frequency, intensity, and duration of physical and mental health problems resulting from the divorce. Significant differences emerged in this regard between contact and disengaged fathers (p<.01). The majority of disengaged fathers experienced stress severe enough to result in the development of new physical and mental health problems: twenty-eight of forty disengaged fathers developed physical symptoms, and thirty-two experienced mental health difficulties after divorce. The majority of contact fathers reported no new physical or mental health problems. Disengaged fathers also indicated a significantly higher level of negative effects on their work or career (p<.01).

Child absence, defined by legal custody and access arrangements and the actual amount of contact between father and child during and after divorce, is experienced differently by contact and disengaged fathers, with disengaged fathers reporting more negative effects. Disengaged fathers, relatively highly involved with and attached to their children before divorce and faced with a dramatic loss of contact within the context of limited access arrangements, experienced the negative effects of their children's absence more acutely than contact fathers (p<.05). For contact fathers, who had been relatively less involved with and attached to their children, adaptation to a "part-time" father-child relationship did not seem to represent the same type of contact loss. "While they experienced child absence, it did not appear to be as problematic an issue asngaged fathers.

The majority of both contact and disengaged fathers identified primarily negative effects of their children's absence. Ten of the twelve fathers not citing solely negative effects were contact fathers. More striking differences between the two groups, however, emerged in the *types* of negative effects identified by fathers, with more disengaged fathers citing depression and a sense of loss in relation to child absence (see Table 19).

**Table 19. Paternal Contact by Negative Effects of
             Child Absence**

Effects	Contact %(N)	Disengaged %(N)	Total % (N)
Depression/sense of loss	24(7)	76(22)	100(29)
Constant worry/yearning for children	53(8)	47(7)	100(15)
Isolation/"emptiness"	67(4)	33(2)	100(6)
Loss of paternal influence/loss of daily routine with children	100(5)	–	100(5)
Generally negative/"bad in every way"	25(1)	75(3)	100(4)
Like death/dying	25(1)	75(3)	100(4)

Table based on the first effect identified by fathers (with a maximum of
three per respondent).
Table listed according to row percentages. Only the most frequently
identified effects are listed.
p<.01

Table 19 suggests that the majority of disengaged fathers, in many instances
well after the divorce, tend to remain at the "depression" stage of the grieving
process. A number of fathers cited two or three major effects of child absence;
of these, disengaged fathers again indicated feelings of depression and a sense of
loss with considerably greater frequency than contact fathers.

Related to child absence is role loss, the loss of a set of functions that
constitute the "father" role. Again, the problems of role loss appeared to be more
pronounced for disengaged fathers. For fathers actively involved with their
children before divorce who defined their identity largely in relation to role as
fathers, when the pre-divorce father-child relationship was perceived to be lost,
so was the paternal role. A clear danger of child absence, as we have seen, is
perceived role loss, leading to further disengagement—the greater the child
absence, the less a father feels that he has a continuing parental role. Child
absence produces a significant change in a father's perception of his function as
a parent: he no longer sees himself as important or valued in that role, which can
lead to eventual disengagement from his children (Greif 1979). Disengaged
fathers did in fact perceive a marked change in their fathering roles during and
after divorce, considering themselves to be significantly less influential in all
major areas of their children's growth and development than did contact fathers,
and rating their post-divorce parenting abilities significantly lower than did

contact fathers (p<.01). Fathers were also asked about their perceptions of their parenting abilities after the divorce. Again differences emerged: while the majority of both groups reported no change in their actual abilities as parents, disengaged fathers were more likely to report a decrease in their abilities and contact fathers more likely to perceive an improvement or no change in their abilities (p<.05).

The third aspect of non-custodial fathers' grief reaction concerns the constraints of the post-divorce "visiting" relationship. Again, for disengaged fathers, "visiting" their children often tended to engender a sense of loss and depression, whereas a number of contact fathers were able to eventually establish a satisfying relationship with their children within these same limitations. The majority of both contact and disengaged fathers identified primarily negative effects of "visiting" (as opposed to "living with") their children, but twelve of the thirteen not citing solely negative effects were contact fathers (p<.01). In regard to the types of negative effects identified by fathers, as with effects of child absence, more disengaged fathers cited depression, a sense of loss, and indicators of continued grief as a result of the constraints of the "visiting" relationship.

In sum, significant differences between contact and disengaged fathers were evident in regard to all three elements of non-custodial fathers' grief reaction—child absence, role loss, and the constraints of the "visiting" relationship—with the theme of depression and a sense of loss being most prevalent among disengaged fathers.

In relation to the effects of divorce on their children, disengaged fathers reported significantly greater perceived negative effects of divorce and father absence (p<.001). The negative effects of father absence were reported more frequently than the more general negative effects of divorce on children. All forty disengaged fathers indicated negative effects of father absence, and twenty-three of forty contact fathers did so. Whereas thirty-two disengaged fathers perceived primarily negative effects of divorce on children, twenty-two contact fathers did so. There were also differences between the two groups in the types of negative effects of father absence identified by fathers (p<.05), with more disengaged fathers citing depression and the fact of their children not being with or knowing their father on a daily basis.

Contact and disengaged fathers were also compared in regard to their perception of the constraints of the "visiting" relationship on their children. Again, disengaged fathers focused on negative effects with much greater frequency than did contact fathers: thirty-five of forty disengaged fathers cited solely negative effects of "visiting" on children, but only sixteen of the forty contact fathers did so (p<.001). There were also significant differences between the two groups in the types of negative effects of the visiting relationship on children (p<.01), with depression, the general pain of the visits, the artificial and strained nature of the visits, and the physical or emotional withdrawal of the child from the father being most frequently mentioned by disengaged fathers.

The differences between contact and disengaged fathers were further reflected in fathers' general assessment of both the problematic and positive aspects of their relationships with their children after divorce. The majority of all fathers identified some negative aspects of the post-divorce father-child relationship, but seven of the eight fathers indicating no negative aspects were contact fathers (p<.05). In listing negative aspects, the most frequently cited was the fact of no contact, mentioned twenty-nine times—all by disengaged fathers. An even more pronounced difference was seen in the positive aspects of the relationship: whereas all forty contact fathers identified some positive aspects, thirty-four of forty disengaged fathers indicated that there were no positive aspects at all in the post-divorce father-child relationship (p<.001).

In sum, the above data on fathers' grief reactions and other internal factors suggest that just as the most "at-risk" group of divorced men are non-custodial fathers of dependent children, so the most vulnerable group of non-custodial fathers appear to be the disengaged fathers. For disengaged fathers with previously intense attachments, divorce is more likely to result in a felt loss, and the grief reaction of these fathers is more acute and prolonged.

Contact fathers with previously less intense attachments, in contrast, are more likely to successfully work through initial difficulties, come to a resolution of their grief, and make a relatively positive transition to divorce. They are eventually able to develop a meaningful relationship with their children within the constraints of "visiting" and thereby report several positive aspects of their post-divorce relationship with their children and, more generally, positive outcomes of the divorce itself.

Two Subgroups of Non-Custodial Fathers

The analysis thus reveals two distinct subgroups of non-custodial fathers, with diametrically opposed patterns of pre- and post-divorce contact with their children: previously involved and attached fathers who became disengaged, and relatively "peripheral" fathers who managed to remain in contact. The majority of the disengaged fathers in the sample consistently scored high on a variety of measures of pre-divorce involvement, attachment, and influence, whereas most contact fathers had relatively low scores on the same indices.

The striking discontinuity between pre- and post-divorce father-child relationship patterns suggests a process involving two interacting components: the *consequences* of divorce and fathers' *adjustment* to these consequences. Consequences can be positive, neutral, or negative, and individuals' adjustment or adaptation will vary accordingly. For previously involved and attached fathers, the consequences of divorce were profound—the loss of the pre-divorce father-child relationship, a relationship that constituted an integral part of their identity. For fathers who were previously less directly involved and attached, the consequences of divorce were less pronounced, and adaptation—the development of a "part-time" parental identity within the confines of a "visiting" relationship—

was not as problematic an issue.

Fathers who located themselves on the "androgynous" or "non-traditional" end of the continuum of pre-divorce fatherhood, when faced with a dramatic loss of contact with their children within the context of limited access arrangements, were more likely to experience the effects of child absence, role loss, and the constraints of the "visiting" relationship in an accurate way. These fathers' adaptation to "non-custodial" status was largely unsuccessful, and the post-divorce outcome was particularly problematic, being marked by chronic grief.

Fathers who defined themselves as peripherally involved with their children before divorce were likely to experience child absence, role loss, and the constraints of a "visiting" relationship less acutely—and in fact may not have been faced with a significant loss of contact with their children during divorce. These previously "traditional" or "breadwinner" fathers often eventually came to enjoy an enhanced level of contact. Improved relationships were possible within the constraints of "visiting" for these fathers; assuming sole responsibility for their children on a limited access basis provided an opportunity to establish more meaningful relationships. Those previously on the "traditional" end of the continuum were thus more likely to remain in contact with their children after divorce and to come to a resolution of their initial grief (see Figure 2).

The key to explaining this finding lies in an understanding of important processes that occur in a relatively brief period during divorce. There is a critical period during which the nature of post-divorce father-child relationships are largely determined: the transition period from the time of divorce (separation) to about six months after, a time when access patterns are established and reinforced. This is also the time when legal processes have their greatest impact, and when multiple adjustments are required on the part of all members of the divorcing family.

During divorce the previously less involved and attached father, faced with perhaps weekend or fortnightly contact in a "visiting" relationship, may find that, with sole responsibility for his children during this time, his fatherhood role can become enhanced. The previously highly involved and attached father, however, faced with diminished contact and what he perceives to be rigid access arrangements, faces a dramatic disentanglement from the routines of daily life with his children—a drastic reduction of contact and role loss which, over a period of time, is a factor in his complete disengagement from the lives of his children.

Positive Outcomes of Divorce

All forty contact fathers clearly indicated at least one positive effect of the divorce on the father-child relationship. Twenty-one contact fathers reported that a closer bond had emerged between their children and themselves after the divorce, and an additional seven indicated a continuing positive relationship. Twelve contact fathers stated that they were "still a father" with a continuing influence in their children's lives. Seven described the luxury of having their children to themselves during access periods, with no "interference" from their spouse, and five indicated that an exposure to two families had important benefits for their children by providing increased support and stimulation. Other positive aspects mentioned were that the father and child had a larger amount of time together than before the divorce, had time of a better quality, the father was becoming more sensitive to his children's feelings and needs, the father was increasingly valuing the relationship, and the children were becoming more independent and self-sufficient.

For many previously "traditional" fathers, divorce represented an opportunity for increased "nurturing" experiences and greater intuitive appreciation of children's growth and development. Mothers no longer functioned as interpreters of children's needs, and fathers could become closer to and more knowledgeable about their children. Further, when marital tensions were chronic, fathers often reported the development of disturbed relationships with their children; in the absence of marital conflicts, much more intimate and warm father-child relationships were possible. With the increase in their direct involvement with and attachment to their children after divorce, many of these fathers reported an improvement in their abilities as parents, with a corresponding change in their conceptions of masculinity and the "father" role:

> My marriage was a traditional one in relation to roles. That's changed for me since the separation, and I'm coping. But in the marriage I was the provider and she was looking after the house and the children—it was very clear-cut (Canadian "contact" father).

> Necessity has made me take on the mother's role while the children are with me—I cook them meals, I bath them, I wash their clothes, I read them bedtime stories (British "contact" father).

Contact fathers were able to adapt flexibly to the constraints of limited access and to work through the complex logistics and specific demands of "visiting" their children. As most contact fathers' pre-divorce roles with their children were limited, the effects of child absence and the constraints of the "visiting" relationship were relatively less problematic. As Wallerstein and Kelly (1980) also found, many fathers indicated that the constraints of limited contact enhanced the father-child relationship, because it was easier for them to function as parents within a circumscribed period. These fathers found the limits of the "visiting" relationship to be more congenial than the daily exposure to (but minimal direct involvement with) their children during the marriage. These

Figure 2. Discontinuity between Pre-Divorce and Post-Divorce Father-Child Relationships

BEFORE DIVORCE	DURING DIVORCE (Transition Period)		AFTER DIVORCE	POST-DIVORCE OUTCOME
"ANDROGYNOUS" FATHERS (Relatively highly involved and attached)	DIMINISHED INVOLVEMENT (Either no contact or contact loss/ threat of loss)	ROLE LOSS	DISENGAGEMENT:	Unsuccessful adaptation to non-custodial status: Chronic grief
"TRADITIONAL" FATHERS Peripherally involved and less attached)	INCREASED INVOLVEMENT (ongoing or increased contact/sole responsibility for children on part time basis)	DEVELOPMENT OF PART-TIME OR "VISITING" FATHERING ROLE	CONTACT:	Successful adaptation to non-custodial status: Resolution of grief

limits helped them to get to know their children better, express affection, and concentrate on their parenting in ways not possible within the marriage. Fathers were less anxious about becoming overwhelmed by the constant demands of their children, as defined access clearly demarcated and limited the interaction. For many contact fathers, the new non-custodial arrangement was much more satisfactory than the "custodial" role within the marriage:

> If my experience is any indication, they become more involved in the day-to-day caring of the child, because when they're with them, they're doing everything, and there's no division of labour, so to speak, because that kind of division of labour in a marriage tends to carry through day in and day out. And probably fathers put the time that they have with their kids higher on the agenda, because that's all there is, they don't see them everyday; they don't take them for granted as much (Canadian "contact" father).

> I think it's good for children to see their fathers in a caring role, rather than a typical family where, although the father might help, most of the responsibility for home and children would fall on the mother. I think it's good for children to see that it can be a shared role. Obviously that happens in some marriages, but in a family where the parents are living apart but still both playing an active and positive role in looking after the children, that sharing of the role is more visible. I think the separation has enhanced my relationship with the children and moved me away from a traditional father role, to one where I share the role of raising the children. I think there's also a change from the children's point of view in that they're more aware of that change in my role, so that they can appreciate better the fact that the father can take on that role as well as the mother (British "contact" father).

In sum, for contact fathers who were on the periphery of their children's lives during the marriage, divorce represents an opportunity to transcend traditional patterns and enhance their relationships with their children within the confines of "visiting." Many non-custodial fathers thus develop, paradoxically, stronger ties to their children than they had before the divorce, being more likely to spend time alone with their children in more intense and meaningful ways.

5

Psychological and Structural Factors Contributing to Disengagement

Most disengaged fathers presented a complex amalgam of reasons for their loss of contact with their children after divorce, rather than one clear cause (see Table 20). Most frequently mentioned (by thirty-six of the forty disengaged fathers) were difficulties related to access, whereas many of the contact fathers stressed the importance of the support and encouragement of their ex-wives in their maintenance of contact and development of a new parental role. Those fathers who received little or no confirmation of their roles as "fathers" by their former spouses appeared most likely to become disengaged from their children's lives.

Table 20. Reasons for Disengagement

Reason	Percentage that Mentioned
Discouragement/denial of access	90(36)
Father's decision to cease contact	33(13)
Practical difficulties (distance, finances, work schedule)	28(11)
Child(ren) not wanting contact	18(7)
Legal injunction	16(6)
Early pattern of no contact (prohibiting future contact)	5(2)

Maximum of three reasons per father.
The numbers in parentheses are the number of fathers responding from the 40-subject disengaged sample.

> That's the way my wife wants it—she doesn't want me around. And it's very difficult for me because I always feel guilty and wonder "Did I try hard enough to get access?" I know I've tried every angle, and there's nothing I can really do now, other than what I've done. And the legal

system has allowed, has encouraged, my wife to cut off contact between me and my son. They say I'm a swine if I don't pay support, but they say nothing about my not being allowed to see my son (Canadian "disengaged" father).

My wife's refusal to share the caring of our son, her perception of him as "her" son and of herself as the only legitimate parent . . . my wife actively breaking off my contact with my son, and her parents' influence in her breaking all ties with me . . . my own inability to see my son on only a sporadic basis, which is nothing like my previous relationship with him or what I think to be fatherhood—tied in with all of this is a tremendous sense of loss, of sadness, of total humiliation and discouragement (British "disengaged" father).

The tension and conflict, the anger that permeated all my contact with my wife and children was impossible to bear. She was really, really angry. Her hands always shook, her voice always trembled—conflict was the central element in our relationship. Each contact involved a major fight, insulting screaming matches where we'd both say really vicious things to each other. It was one huge trauma for the girls. We'd argue and fight, I'd take my daughters, brood all afternoon, come back, and there'd be another big scene. My daughters would listen to this; they'd cry and scream. My wife threatened to call the police; I was in a blind fury. Finally I gave up—it was hopeless. My daughter was in the middle, she was unhappy, wetting the bed. You have the kid's welfare at heart, which my wife used as a convenient weapon against me. She saw me as causing all this damage, as the disruptive influence in my daughter's life. So the solution is to remove this disruptive influence. I was told to stay away, that I was harmful emotionally to my children. But never mind my daughter's constant pleas for her dad, never mind my wife telling my daughter that I had abandoned her. These are all subtle things that my wife wouldn't admit even to herself, but they're what determined the final outcome. After awhile I became afraid to make contact. My wife was perfectly content not to have me re-enter the children's life: that becomes a tremendous barrier—you become afraid of making contact. After awhile you rebuild your life, they rebuild theirs—it becomes easier to accept the status quo (Canadian "disengaged" father).

Linked to ex-wives' lack of support for paternal contact and fathers' feelings of no longer being influential and valued as fathers, were fathers' own decisions to cease contact with their children. The thirteen fathers who citied this reason spoke of their overwhelming sense of loss and depression, the pain of seeing their children only intermittently, and the fact that an avuncular "visiting" relationship in no sense resembled "real fatherhood" and was perhaps harmful for children as well. Fathers' own decisions to cease contact were inextricably linked to their inability to adapt to the constraints of the "visiting" relationship:

> The most difficult thing is not seeing them and not actually being there to see them grow up. If you don't see them for three months or six months or whatever, you've missed six months of their life. You've missed the wee things like, "Dad, the ice-cream van's here" or "Dad, I've got homework to do" or this and that. And then you've got to say goodbye to them, and it's very frustrating. And you wonder—I still don't really know what's best—I wonder if maybe it would be better to leave them alone and let them live their life, and it's not knowing what to do, not knowing which is best for them. The feeling you get inside yourself everytime you go away: "Am I doing the right thing by seeing them, would they be better off if I just didn't see them?"—it's basically just a hurtful relationship. There's a lot of men who really care about their kids but walk away from them because there's too much hurt on both sides. But a lot of people don't realize that. I used to be one of them, by the way, who thought really badly about a father who hadn't seen his kids in years. People seemingly label these fathers as uncaring people, but sometimes I wonder if in fact they're more caring, because of the hurt involved, and the separation. And each time you've got your child and your child has to go back is really hard, is really difficult. And until you go through it, you can't understand it. And I think especially with younger kids, the quicker a parent doesn't see their kids then their kids aren't really realizing that their dad's not there. Maybe it's less hurtful because both the child and parent have to say goodbye to each other, and both of you are practically in tears. There's a sort of silence between you—it's like continual hurt. And men that don't actually go and see their kids again, I quite admire, because they're minimizing the pain on that child, because otherwise it's continual pain. But the pain never goes away for the father, no matter what he does (British "disengaged" father).

> Mainly that I couldn't accept the role of simply being a visitor in my kids' lives. I'd been so involved with them, when I lived with them, as a father, that the gulf between simply being somebody who's a visitor, who took them out occasionally, and being a father, was just too wide for me to bridge. And I also felt that it would inevitably lead to resentment on their part about it. I didn't think that I could cope during the time that I did see them as a visitor . . . and that probably during the whole of that time I'd be screwed up emotionally to such an extent that

that would convey itself to them, and lead to them not wanting to be with me (Canadian "disengaged" father).

Eleven fathers mentioned practical difficulties in exercising access, including problems of distance, transportation, finances, work schedule, or lack of adequate accommodation, but only as a secondary factor in their loss of contact. Seven referred to a lack of confirmation of the non-custodial father role by their children, or their children increasingly distancing themselves from their father after divorce; six mentioned the bias of the legal system towards sole maternal custody and the existence of a legal injunction prohibiting the type of contact they had desired; and two fathers indicated that they had been unable to overcome a pattern of diminished or no contact established in the months immediately following divorce.

Clearly, a shortcoming of the study is that only fathers' own stated reasons for disengagement were assessed; corroborative information from other members of the divorced family was not available, and uncritical reliance on self-report data can be problematic as fathers tended to largely underestimate their own role in their loss of contact with their children. Nevertheless, fathers' own interpretations of the disengagement process, not previously examined in the divorce literature, are what they face and act upon. For this reason, any analysis of paternal disengagement must begin with and seriously consider fathers' self-reports. There were many indications in the data, however, that paternal disengagement is a much more complex phenomenon than merely the result of obstruction of access by the former spouse.

Interdependence of Structural and Psychological Factors

A closer scrutiny of the dynamics underlying the process of disengagement suggests that two orders of variables determine the level of post-divorce father-child contact: structural and psychological. The disengagement of non-custodial fathers after divorce is a result of a combination of structural constraints and fathers' own psychological responses to the perceived loss of their children. On its own, each factor is usually insufficient to effect disengagement; combined, the two are a potent force militating against post-divorce paternal contact. Both structural and psychological factors are critical mediating variables between divorce and disengagement. Divorce represents a situation where a father is judicially, culturally, and legislatively disadvantaged on the basis of gender, but a father's psychological adjustment to the consequences of divorce is the other critical factor in the disengagement equation.

Non-custodial fathers' disengagement from their children should not be interpreted as a lack of interest in their children, or the end result of what may have been a tenuous father-child relationship during the marriage. The grief of previously highly involved (and now disengaged) fathers is the most pronounced and remains unresolved: chronic grief is most characteristic of this group, a reflection of their closer attachment to their children before divorce. Psychological factors related to fathers' unresolved grief and inability to adapt to child absence, role loss, and the constraints of the "visiting" relationship are highly significant in their eventual disengagement. Fathers' lack of help-seeking behaviour further compounds the resolution of grief associated with the multiple losses experienced with a divorce.

It also cannot be assumed that fathers' post-divorce roles are solely reflections of their choices. Highly involved and attached fathers during the marriage are highly vulnerable in relation to structural constraints and the effects of a judicial mode of custody and access determination, often being caught in a seemingly insoluble dilemma. Unable to tolerate the idea of the loss of their children but given little expectation for success and what many consider to be a highly adversarial means to try to prevent the loss (which they believe will seriously harm their children), they gradually disengage from their children's lives. Such fathers, often unaware of alternatives in custody and access resolution and post-divorce custody arrangements at the time of divorce, rarely make legal application for custody, although they are the most likely to desire at least partial physical custody of their children. Structural factors, delineating and regulating the boundaries of the post-divorce father-child relationship, are thus also significant determinants of fathers' subsequent loss of contact with their children. Existing analyses of "divorce adjustment" have overlooked this dynamic interaction between the structural consequences of divorce for non-custodial fathers and individual fathers' psychological adaptation to these consequences. The concept of "divorce adjustment" prevalent in the divorce research suggests that it is *individuals* who are expected to come to terms with (or adjust to) the consequences of divorce; the social structure is not implicated as in need of fundamental change.

Structural Factors

Adversarial Nature of Legal Processes

Disengaged fathers identified the antagonistic nature of the post-divorce relationship between the former spouses as resulting in withheld access, which was identified as the primary barrier to their post-divorce contact with their children. Our data suggest that legal processes are strongly implicated in exacerbating or creating such conflict and hence in paternal disengagement. Assessment of lawyers in helping or hindering their subsequent relationships with their children, and of the judicial system in regard to its appropriateness as a forum for determining child custody and access arrangements, differed between contact and disengaged fathers. Disengaged fathers felt that the system of individual representation characteristic of the traditional adversarial approach of the legal system had polarized the divorcing spouses. They felt the provocative behaviour of lawyers and the adversarial nature of the legal system often created overt conflict where little such antagonism had previously existed. Direct communication between spouses was usually prohibited by the lawyers of either or both parties, and a more hostile tone was introduced via letters and affidavits drafted by lawyers but ostensibly representing their clients' sentiments, which constituted a new medium of communication between the "plaintiff," or "pursuer," and "defendant."

> They brewed up bad feelings between my wife and myself—the letters that the lawyers have sent us—one trying to intimidate the other. My wife was boiling over a letter written by my lawyer which I knew nothing about, and I was really mad about a letter her lawyer sent me. It's been made into a war (British "disengaged" father).

> A woman goes to her lawyer and says, "Look, I'm not getting along with this guy, I'm frustrated, I'm fed up," or whatever, and her lawyer then says, "What a rotten swine," and then they write up a great big affidavit that accuses the father of being the rottenest son-of-a-bitch on this earth. And that's presented to the father, and the father sees this, but it's not worded in the wife's words, it's worded by the lawyer, and they get madder than hell when they see all this nonsense. And then they go and see their lawyer and their lawyer reads this and then he writes up a whole bunch of crap back. So that's the big thump—that's what kills it, right then and there, then it's a big fight all the way in (Canadian "disengaged" father).

> They essentially produced a negative tone in the relationship where none existed before. Essentially the adversarial principle produces hostility where there might have been compromise. It results in not being able to do things spontaneously which you would do in a normal relationship—it causes you not to telephone, it causes you not to write. If you do write it is through the lawyer to another lawyer. It makes contact very formal, including contact with children, which is not a natural way of relating. It restricts contact to a particular time, day, or time of year. There is no spontaneity left in the relationship. But the worst thing it does is divide you into two sides and there's no middle ground or common ground which is where we'd normally be. Essentially you have no communication with your wife about the children since everything is filtered through lawyers (British "disengaged" father).

From the research evidence available, it is clear that most lawyers approach divorce in a traditional adversarial manner (Eekelaar 1984) and consider that in being partisan and assuming a "fighting" posture they are merely protecting their client's interests (Murch 1980). The assumption that because two individuals are divorcing they are necessarily in conflict is prevalent (Murch 1980). However, a sizeable proportion of fathers in the present study did not report a situation of high conflict between the spouses at the time of the separation, before legal consultation, and a third of the fathers who had expressed a desire for at least partial physical custody of their children reported no overt disagreement between the spouses over child custody at that time. These fathers believed that the possibility of some type of shared custody arrangement clearly existed at the point of separation:

> We originally had a joint custody agreement, and it was the legal system that tore this apart, it destroyed it. We had agreed beforehand and then this happened—the legal system intervened (Canadian "disengaged" father).

> Joint custody was a very real possibility in my mind at that time. It seems to me now that by listening to the lawyer and agreeing to grant sole custody to my wife, that it jeopardized my future relationship with my daughter. My lawyer kept stressing that the most important thing was to make the terms of the property settlement easier—and to do this I would have to agree to my wife having sole custody. . . . Basically I sacrificed custody in the interests of a property settlement (Canadian "disengaged" father).

Many disengaged fathers described feeling intimidated by the adversarial approach of the legal system and were cognizant of the dangers of this type of approach for their children's well-being, another significant factor in their decision not to legally contest the issue of custody. Only 15 of the 80 fathers legally contested custody via the courts, despite the fact that 63 (or 79 percent) had expressed a desire for at least partial physical custody of their children at the time of the divorce. Fathers generally conceived of a custody "battle" as an attack: defence in order to impress the judge, with detailed accounts of neglect, abuse, and other accusations presented by both sides in their attempt to "win" their children. Many saw contested custody as more likely to hurt their children (and former spouses) than to facilitate the development of a meaningful post-divorce relationship with their children. Indeed, their overriding concern was that their children would be used as "pawns" and "weapons" in the "battle" that would likely continue well after the custody hearing:

The way the lawyers fight—tit for tat all the time. It's made into a battle, it's bargaining for a human life. It's made worse since the law leans toward the mother in the case of custody. The mother says "The law is on my side," and I as the father am forced to fight, which I don't want to do (British "disengaged" father).

My wife and I had no opportunity to come face-to-face to discuss our situation—everything transpired between the lawyers. My wife decided to obtain sole custody through the court, and my lawyer felt that I needed to take a "fighting" posture. My wife certainly used her lawyer this way, which led to a very acrimonious situation. My wife's lawyer prevented me from having contact with my children, so that after two or three months when I finally did see my children, they were visibly scared when they did see me, and were quite reluctant to go out with me. My wife's lawyer used this in court later on (British "disengaged" father).

I continued my efforts toward a reconciliation, mainly by trying to be patient, remaining where I was, patient, in total desolation. I couldn't act in any kind of positive way—I had to endure my suffering in the right way, with integrity. Any action that I could have taken—bringing Michael home with me against my wife's wishes, consulting a lawyer, fighting a custody battle in court—I considered all of these as violent means, which ethically I couldn't do. I thought only about preserving my integrity and enduring it all in the right way—although I admit I cut quite a ridiculous figure in the process (British "disengaged" father).

Many disengaged fathers considered contested custody, and the use of the legal process generally, as a highly adversarial means that did not justify the end they were seeking. These fathers described themselves as strongly and intimately attached to their children and were primarily concerned with the potential harmful effects of the adversarial process on their children. For these fathers, however, withdrawal from the adversarial process further jeopardized their ongoing contact with their children, as the level of hostility between the spouses engendered by the legal process was that negotiation had effectively become an impossibility.

Feelings of powerlessness and victimization were prevalent among disengaged fathers who, throughout the time of legal negotiation, attempted to maintain their pre-existing bond with their children by not using what they perceived to be an adversarial approach to "win" custody. Their lawyers (or ex-wives' lawyers) nevertheless adopted adversarial means in the legal negotiations that took place. Engaged in an adversarial process but not wanting to use such means to "win" custody, those fathers who expressed a strong desire for a shared physical custody arrangement after divorce were viewed with suspicion and their desires and motives were questioned. They were assumed to not genuinely want the burden of full or shared custody but to have ulterior motives in positing such a "threat" or "bluff." In reality, their previous involvement with and attachment to their children made them unable to wage a public "fight," which they perceived would harm their children. Their refusal to adopt such means, however, contributed to their loss of contact with their children.

Disengaged fathers often saw their lawyers (and the legal "divorce industry") as having a vested interest in profiting financially from ongoing conflict and hence less likely to be alert to the possibilities of reconciliation or reaching an amicable settlement by means of non adversarial negotiation or mediation. Fathers described lawyers' tactical manoeuvres towards exacerbating and perpetuating conflict between the former spouses as manipulative and designed to extract financial profit from the breakdown of their clients' family relationships. These fathers came to resent their escalating dependence on their lawyers and the legal system. However, they felt "locked into" the legal process insofar as they had lost trust in their ex-wives, felt vulnerable in terms of their future relationship with their children, and needed the special protection of a lawyer. This loss of trust between the spouses and feelings of vulnerability were seen by fathers to have been deliberately engineered by their lawyers and a legal framework that actively promoted such a dependency. In this context, fathers spoke of the slowness and constant delays of the legal machinery and of high legal costs as largely unnecessary.

> The law acts so slowly, and emotional matters should be resolved quickly if there's going to be a balanced outcome. For example, it took six weeks for the fact of non-access to be brought into the court and a further three weeks for it to be dealt with—a total of nine weeks of non-contact had elapsed. The law delays things a lot as well as polarizing parental opinions (British "disengaged" father).

Finally, disengaged fathers stressed that the use of legal tactics appropriate to the "combat" of litigation, when applied insensitively to issues arising from emotional difficulties in family relationships, could be highly damaging. The judicial system was thus considered by all disengaged fathers to be an inappropriate forum for resolving issues of child custody and access.

> The whole system is totally barbaric—it is not in the least interested in the children's welfare, as I found out in that court. It's just to get a decision made—they're there to make a decision but unqualified to make the decision, and more often than not they make the wrong decision, because they do not know the family's circumstances, without liaising or consulting with any member of the family. It's the judge's decision, which I find farcical (British "disengaged" father).

Identified by fathers as primarily responsible for their loss of contact with their children was the obstruction of access by the former spouse. Clearly, the less supportive that a custodial mother is towards paternal access, the greater the likelihood of access difficulties and eventual disengagement of the father. The *source* of ex-wives' hostility to post-divorce father-child contact thus becomes an important question. Interspousal hostility after divorce is not necessarily primarily influenced by pre-divorce patterns. Through mistrust and anger are almost universally present in varying degrees upon divorce, intensified conflict during and after divorce may be directly related to intervening legal processes. Fathers frequently held their lawyers and the legal system responsible for exacerbating or creating conflict between the spouses. Many fathers initially made attempts to discuss terms of custody and access directly with their wives but were restrained by their lawyers (as were their wives) from communicating directly and were instructed to negotiate through their respective lawyers. Negotiations that involved lawyers acting as intermediaries typically lasted at least several months or, for many, several years, during which an atmosphere of competition, fear, and mistrust prevailed over what was reported by some fathers as a spirit of cooperation (despite disagreements) at the time of divorce with regard to post-divorce arrangements for the children. The adversarial nature of legal processes, whether restricted to negotiations between lawyers or involving court action, makes it highly unlikely that a spirit of friendship and cooperation will survive the divorce. Severe conflict is the end result of a negotiating environment that effectively forces each party to assume an extreme position.

To test the influence of legal processes in exacerbating or creating post-divorce spousal conflict, the level of conflict between the spouses at the time of separation (before any major legal involvement) was compared with the post-divorce level of friendliness between the former spouses (after legal processes had made their major impact). No correlation was found between the level of interspousal conflict at the time of the divorce and the nature of ex-spouses' post-divorce contact; that is, the likelihood of friendly and unfriendly (or non-existent) post-divorce contact did not depend on the level of conflict between spouses at the time of divorce—suggesting the presence of mediating factors operating in the period during divorce that influence the nature of the subsequent relationship.

As detailed in chapter 4, there was also no association between the level of conflict between the spouses at the time of divorce (separation) and subsequent father-child contact: conflict between the spouses *upon separation* did not necessarily lead to paternal disengagement. The relationship between paternal contact and the level of conflict between the parents *after divorce*, however, was highly significant (p<.001). Post- but not pre-divorce parental conflict was associated with non-custodial fathers' disengagement from their children. This further suggests that mediating factors are at work during divorce to produce a level of parental conflict strong enough to result in access difficulties for non-custodial fathers, followed by eventual loss of contact.

Significantly, most disengaged fathers described their ex-wives as having believed in fathers' ability to be effective parents, as having confidence in and generally agreeing with fathers' child-rearing practices during the marriage. Disagreements over child-related matters within the marriage were reported as relatively rare. The fact that the great majority of divorces involve two capable and loving parents could be used as the basis for developing positive co-parental relationships after divorce. In contrast, within the legal process, former spouses are oriented towards devaluing the relative contribution of the other. Distorted perceptions of the former spouse appear to be a frequent result of a legal mode of custody and access resolution. Up to the time of legal negotiations, each parent has usually viewed the other as necessary to the children's lives; the adversarial stance adopted during legal negotiations contributes to a dramatic shift in this perception.

Child Custody Determination

Traditional access arrangements were considered to be entirely inadequate by disengaged fathers who perceived themselves as highly involved with their children before divorce. At the time of the divorce, the great majority of these fathers had wanted at least partial *physical* custody of their children. They described their actual custody and access arrangements as woefully insufficient. The main issue for these fathers was not *legal* custody and access per se, rather, they were primarily concerned with maintaining a meaningful post-divorce relationship with their children in the form of regular and frequent physical contact.

Disengaged fathers yearned for the children with whom they were no longer in contact. All forty disengaged fathers indicated a desire for "a lot more" contact with their children (see Table 21).

Table 21. Paternal Contact by Desired Level of Child Contact after Divorce

	Contact %(N)	Disengaged %(N)	Total % (N)
A lot more	40(16)	100(40)	70(56)
Some more	28(11)	–	14(11)
About right	30(12)	–	15(12)
A little less	2(1)	–	1(1)
Total	100(40)	100(40)	100(80)

p<.001

Existing divorce literature, though containing little empirical data about fathers' desired level of contact with their children after divorce, often contains suggestions that fathers simply do not want custody of their children and explains fathers' disengagement primarily in terms of a lack of interest (Eekelaar and Clive 1977). The findings of this study suggest otherwise. The great majority of non-custodial fathers considered traditional legal access arrangements to be insufficient and wanted at least partial physical custody. This was most evident in the case of disengaged fathers. Dissatisfaction with existing legal custody and access arrangements, and with actual physical arrangements, was highest among non-custodial fathers who had previously enjoyed a relatively high level of involvement, attachment, and influence and had subsequently lost all contact with their children.

The discrepancy between fathers' desires for custody and access and actual post-divorce arrangements is striking. Seventy-nine percent of all the non-custodial fathers and 88 percent of the disengaged fathers in the sample indicated that, at the time of the divorce, their preferred arrangement was one in which their children could live with them at least part of the time, including overnight stays. Clearly, fathers who legally disputed custody and forced a court decision (fifteen of eighty fathers) were not all of those who wanted custody of their children; powerful factors appeared to be mediating between fathers' stated desires at the time of divorce and the final outcome of paternal non-custody, and between these desires and fathers' subsequent inaction towards the pursuit of custody.

The role of lawyers was crucial in transforming fathers' aspirations regarding what they could achieve through the legal system. Lawyers assumed a key role in persuading fathers not to pursue custody or lessening their aspirations concerning their level of post-divorce contact with their children. In 55 percent of cases, lawyers actively discouraged fathers from pursuing custody; only 12 percent agreed with or encouraged it. Fathers were often told that a "reasonable" amount of post-divorce contact was the "customary" pattern of fortnightly access. In a field that relies heavily on precedent for its decisions, it has been convenient and comfortable to recommend what has gone before. The precedents of maternal custody and twice-monthly paternal access have become, in the eyes of lawyers and the judiciary, not only customary, but somehow developmentally and morally correct (Felner et al. 1985). Fathers wanting custody or open access to their children are viewed with suspicion; mothers who wish to accommodate such fathers are advised not to "give up" too much (Felner et al. 1985). For non-custodial fathers, the pattern of "visiting" their children on a weekly or fortnightly basis—often, at best, two days out of every fourteen—has thus continued, despite fathers' strong dissatisfaction with the limited nature of such contact, children's yearning for increased contact with their fathers, and mothers often feeling overwhelmed by the sole responsibility for their children after divorce.

Lawyers play a central role in providing their clients with a basic knowledge of the law and legal processes, helping them to decide what to ask for, and shaping expectations of what they will get. If lawyers' advice regarding post-divorce contact is discouraging, it is likely that fathers will lower their expectations; if the expectation that the best fathers can hope for is limited access, these expectations shape what fathers strive for—and settle for. Given that most custody and access arrangements only reach the court as a fait accompli, the way in which lawyers advise their clients is an important determinant of the final structural arrangements made. What lawyers advise is influenced by what they think the court will accept ("bargaining in the shadow of the law"). The majority of fathers, faced with explicit advice and strong direction from their lawyers towards maternal custody with limited parental access, and convinced on the basis of judicial precedent that they have a limited chance of success through the courts, eventually accept the predominant pattern of weekly or fortnightly "visiting":

> I got the impression that there would be no problem getting access, getting Andrew to stay with me on weekends and so on, but it didn't work out that way. He also told me that I should forget about custody, and to just concentrate on access, which I now realize was wrong (Canadian "disengaged" father).

> The lawyer advised me to give the mother interim custody and not to worry about it or fight it. I didn't know at that time that in fact, when you're talking about custody, nothing is "interim"—anything that is "interim" means that it is forever. I didn't know that at that time (Canadian "disengaged" father).

> Initially when there's a separation, there should be someplace to go to try to save a relationship, rather than turning to lawyers and finding out what you're going to get and what you're not going to get through a divorce. The legal system makes things happen that should never happen—it calls for no effort on the part of the husband or wife. It's presented as the easiest, as the only, alternative. Fathers are told that they should just give up the idea of custody—there's nothing positive fathers can do—and mothers are told that they'll get everything, they're entitled to it, and that the lawyers will get it all for them. For fathers a sense of resignation starts when lawyers tell them that they don't have a chance for keeping the same relationship they had with their children before they separated, and all kinds of other people—society generally—supports this view. It completely takes over as time goes on and fathers realize that the whole situation is hopeless. And they're left feeling completely helpless (Canadian "disengaged" father).

By preadjudicating custody disputes on the basis of anticipations of what would happen were the dispute to be carried to court, lawyers perpetuate the (perceived) maternal custody bias of the judiciary. Inaction because of an assumption of prejudice becomes a self-fulfilling prophecy and reinforces the status quo. The feeling that fathers are at a severe disadvantage in relation to custody of their children in the courts is widespread:

> They don't give men the benefit of the possibility that they may be good parents. They look at you as if you're doing something wrong, as if you're the guilty party. Lawyers and judges are the mainstay of the problems that men and children have, when it comes to men and children not having the right to maintain their relationship. And they support women if they decide to break the relationship—they promote women's anger and bitterness, and promote destruction of the father-child relationship. Before the separation, I had faith in the legal system. I've been through it and now find myself with no confidence in the system whatsoever. I believe in the truth, and I couldn't believe how full of lies the whole legal system is (Canadian "disengaged" father).

If a father does not accept his lawyer's advice and seeks to challenge traditional custody and access arrangements, his lawyer may refuse to proceed with the application or to represent his client, or, if he "agrees" to contest custody, the father's case may not be presented strongly. The difficulty of obtaining legal aid for an action that is unlikely to succeed is endemic for divorcing fathers, while private litigants may be deterred by prohibitive legal costs (Parkinson 1987). When custody is contested, as was the case with fifteen men in the study, fathers and their lawyers are faced with a judiciary that is seen to act according to a maternal presumption, despite the gender-neutral standard of "the best interests of the child." The main issue in contested cases, under the rubric of "the best interests of the child," is seen to be the tolerable fitness of the mother, above all other factors. In fact, the outcome of contested cases of child custody, regardless of whom children are living with at the time of the hearing or of pre-divorce parenting patterns, continues to be, in the great majority of cases, a maternal custody determination. These contested cases define legal norms and form the basis of a body of law upon which all divorced fathers are advised.

Custody determinations made by the courts, influencing the type of advice offered to fathers by lawyers, appear to be largely based on the assumption of fathers' primary role as economic providers for their children, and secondary role as caretakers. The nature of the pre-divorce father-child relationship does not appear to be a significant factor in legal custody outcomes. Lawyers' directions rarely differ for divorced fathers: sole maternal custody with limited paternal access was almost universally recommended for the fathers in the sample. However, a heterogeneity of fathering roles exists among families. Even though both highly and peripherally involved and attached fathers received the same advice from their lawyers regarding custody and access, the satisfaction of each group with final custody and access arrangements and the level of their post-divorce contact with their children was radically different. This uniformity of approach among lawyers and the generally unvarying nature of the judicial resolution of custody and access for fathers with vastly different patterns and experiences of fatherhood may be largely responsible for the poor outcome for those fathers who had been more involved with and attached to their children during the marriage. Fathers enter the legal process with very different pre-divorce father-child relationship patterns. Such heterogeneity warrants against a homogeneous approach, yet the legal process, bound by precedent, structures post-divorce relationships according to largely fixed rules that ensure that the "motherhood" and fatherhood" mandates remain intact.

As argued in Chapter 2, the state has a strong interest in the maintenance of appropriate work and family role behaviours. Upon divorce, the judicial system plays a central role in limiting child custody and access options, sanctioning and legitimizing traditional structures and relationships, and perpetuating a gender-based division of roles in the post-divorce family. The "motherhood" and "fatherhood" mandates are clear: the father remains responsible for children's economic support, the mother for their care. Thus we see a consistent pattern of decisions that justify and reinforce a maternal presumption; this judicially constructed preference has operated as effectively as a statutory directive (Weitzman 1985; Foote 1988).

Psychological Factors

Grieving Process

The intensity of the pre-divorce father-child relationship and its interactions is of paramount importance in determining the outcome of the grieving process of non-custodial fathers. Those fathers most involved with and attached to their children before divorce are most likely to experience acutely the negative effects of the loss or absence of their children and are the group most at risk of losing contact with their children following divorce.

With a startling intensity, the disengaged fathers in the sample described being emotionally connected to their children in strong and intimate ways, defining their "fathering" role as a central component of their identity:

> Definitions of fathering vary tremendously but I personally would equate it with parenting: a complete commitment to one's child, the major responsibility in one's life, a combination of nurturance, encouraging autonomy and initiative within prescribed limits. It's setting the stage to allow a child to grow and develop his potential to the maximum (British "disengaged" father).

It means having an ongoing and continuing interest in the child's welfare during their life, even if they're doing things of which you don't approve. It means, on the one hand, being available when there are crises and difficult questions, and on the other hand being able to stand back a little and let the young person get a degree of independence. To make the young person value themselves as an individual and not just a clone of mother and father. It also includes a lot of physical things—washing sheets, ironing, making sausages. It means sharing things and sharing tasks, particularly when the wife is also doing a part- or a full-time job (British "disengaged" father).

It's a way of living—getting up with your children, eating with them, doing work together, reading with them, hugging them, putting them to sleep, dealing with their fears, and enjoying their pleasures—living with them (British "disengaged" father).

Contributing to the chronic grief of disengaged fathers is the fact that while a salient loss has occurred, the object of their grief is very much alive, and the grieving process persists. The predominant feature of the chronic grief of disengaged fathers is a pervasive sense of preoccupation, loss, and sadness. Depressive features are most often cited in fathers' descriptions of their post-divorce relationship with their children:

I think of them everyday, almost constantly, although I never see them. I feel I am constantly searching for my children, I think I see their faces in other children's faces. It's a desperate kind of yearning (British "disengaged" father).

I have a constant, very real pain in my chest; there's tension, lack of sleep, constant worry. . . . I'm totally preoccupied with my son, and a lot of my time is spent trying not to think about what happened. But mainly it's a feeling of sadness, an emptiness, a kind of darkness (Canadian "disengaged" father).

I feel depressed and alone. At times I have a total feeling of despair, but I've got to gear my thoughts away from thinking like that. My heart feels like it's been ripped away, but I try to consciously steer myself away from thinking like that. I have to put on a facade of coping (British "disengaged" father).

I'm finding it impossible to adjust. I had a big part of my life that I enjoyed—and lived for—just taken away. I feel a big gap in my life that I can't fill. I feel that the less I see of him the further away I'm getting from him. But the strain of seeing him for just a few hours a week was too much not only for me but on my son's side as well. The house is like a morgue—it's completely quiet, completely cold. I've felt very depressed but just have had to accept the fact that I've lost him and can't do anything about it. I've just had to accept the fact that I'm no longer part of his life. . . . I felt like a rat trapped in a cage. I felt on the verge of violence. I wanted to strike out against every member of her family. I felt paranoid—like I was falling apart, piece by piece. I couldn't concentrate on things—on anything, really. I felt mainly depressed after awhile—completely confused and hopeless after trying to think over what had happened and why it happened. Just a deep sadness about my son and about what had happened (British "disengaged" father).

Depression, a sense of being unable to help those that I love, a sense of worry about what's going on with the children, a sense of helplessness that the people I love the most I can't help, a sense of utter horror at what society is doing in requiring a father to go through horrendous long legal proceedings just to get permission to see his children, much less have any kind of normal father-child relationship (Canadian "disengaged" father).

Child Absence

Child absence produces a significant difference in fathers' perceptions of their functioning as parents after divorce. Feeling devalued as parents, previously highly involved and attached fathers described themselves as being rootless, having no structure in their lives, and generally anxious, helpless, and depressed. Actively involved in their children's care and upbringing within the marriage and deriving much satisfaction from parental tasks, these fathers had largely transcended the traditional "fatherhood mandate." They consistently referred to initial fears of a diminished relationship with their children, and to subsequent preoccupation with the absence of their children. Feeling deeply attached to their children during the marriage, they saw themselves as primary nurturers or at least co-nurturers of their children, and they could not, upon divorce, tolerate the idea that this function was in jeopardy.

Although child absence manifested itself in a number of ways, the great majority of disengaged fathers in the sample displayed signs of depression, resignation, and a full grief reaction connected to the loss of their children:

It's a very great loss. It makes me sad, I have periods of intermittent depression, I wake up at 4:00 a.m., I have a lot of sleepless nights. Of course my present wife has helped tremendously, and encouraged me to channel these feelings into positive endeavors. But there's a tremendous feeling of loss and sadness, and it's a loss which can never be regained. The period of a child's life growing, in Elspeth's case, from 8 to 14, is a vital period for her and a vital period for me, which has been lost forever (British "disengaged" father).

I feel very bad—I feel I am lost with nowhere to go, with no direction. And I feel no one can save me; I don't know how I can survive like this. I can't sleep—all the time I think about them (Canadian "disengaged" father).

Terrible. It's a piece of my life that's missing. There's not a day in my life that she does not enter my thoughts, in one way or another. It's a tremendous sense of loss that I'm left with—constantly (Canadian "disengaged" father).

I feel numb, I don't feel anything anymore. At first I felt completely terrified, for about 4 years. And then I just started losing all feeling. I don't know what I feel right now (Canadian "disengaged" father).

The impact of child absence seemed to be as potent for those fathers who had not seen their children for several years as for those who had lost contact more recently. Time elapsed since the divorce, or since the last contact with their children, did not appear to diminish the intensity of the fathers' grief.

Role Loss

Child absence is accompanied by role loss. Despite the fact that a "real" loss of children occurs after divorce, fathers also lose the status or role of "fatherhood," which for previously highly involved fathers is a major integrative force in their day-to-day functioning and an important component of their identity and status. As the child is lost, so is the "father" role with its functions and privileges.

Disengaged fathers, having enjoyed a relatively active pre-divorce "fathering" role, found it almost impossible to maintain their roles as parents in the face of limited contact and felt they had a significantly decreased level of influence in all areas of their children's growth and development. The less opportunity fathers had to act as "fathers," the less they saw themselves as "fathers." Role loss can lead to retreatism (Merton 1968). The most previously involved and attached fathers, when faced with child absence and perceived role loss, feel their ability and confidence in their "fathering" role to be drastically undermined:

Whereas I know I displayed confidence and skill in rearing my child before the separation, I feel quite uncomfortable around young children now. Even after a few days of being separated from my son, I initially felt anxious and awkward when I did see him and he reacted also in an awkward fashion. I very much question my abilities now, although I still feel a great yearning to be a parent and to utilize the talents I know I have. I just feel a tremendous lack in my life (British "disengaged" father).

I don't really think I have parenting abilities now because I don't live with them. A parent should be a person that's there all the time. Now it's just like seeing someone that you care about, but only during certain periods, certain times—it's not really being a parent. To be a parent you've got to actually be there as they're growing up, and I haven't done that in the last few years. At best I'm just a friend (British "disengaged" father).

Parkes (1986) and others have identified the creation of a new identity as crucial in the resolution of the grieving process. This was particularly problematic in cases where a father's identity was largely defined by his relationship with his child. Further, the father-child relationship meets the needs for nurture, affection, love, and status for both father and child; children satisfy longings for genetic immortality, intimacy, and family life—this too is lost after divorce. As Erikson (1959), argues, "generativity" is a critical stage of the growth of the healthy adult personality, and "regression from generativity" results in a sense of stagnation and interpersonal impoverishment.

The "Visiting" Relationship

An important psychological barrier to non-custodial fathers' post-divorce contact with their children is their inability to adapt to the constraints of the "visiting" relationship and to construct a new role as "part-time" parent after divorce. This was a particularly significant component in the disengagement of fathers who had had an active role to play in their children's lives during the marriage. Highly involved and attached fathers face the most abrupt disentanglement from the routines and events of day-to-day life that had structured their parenting role, amd their ongoing relationship is severely restricted by the legally determined patterns and constraints of access "visits."

Disengaged fathers' conceptions of what "fatherhood" constituted were diametrically opposed to the structure that had been imposed upon them. For these fathers, "real fatherhood" meant living with their children on a full-time basis and sharing in everyday life with them. They felt "confused" and "lost" without their children with them on a full-time basis. They had a particularly strong desire to continue to be influential in all aspects of their children's growth and development, values and lifestyle, which they found difficult or impossible to do within the constraints of "visiting."

Confirming the findings of Wallerstein and Kelly (1980), the pain of the visits—their brevity, artificiality, and superficiality—exacerbated fathers' sense of loss. Access visits symbolized the abrupt ending of the pre-divorce father-child relationship and emphasized what had been lost in the divorce—the loss of their children and the daily routine that had previously sustained the relationship.

For previously involved and attached fathers, "visiting" their children mainly exacerbated already-intense feelings of loss and deprivation:

> I find that visiting is very hard. The time is very restricted, the constant burden of a limited, restricted time is a very great pressure. There's a constant feeling that they're not your own any more—you try to fight off this feeling, you feel very emotional about it (British "disengaged" father).

> Living with would be so much easier than visiting, if I had the opportunity to do so. Visiting was very, very stressful, extremely upsetting. The changeover in my own case was very, very difficult, because of constraints put upon the children by my wife and her parents. Things weren't made easy because of comments from my mother-in-law or my wife. It was very cold, unfeeling. If I were living with them, there'd be more time to establish a father role, more chance of a bonding, of a better bonding (British "disengaged" father).

> I think visiting is just a tease. It's frustrating and it's unsatisfying, and it's not a normal father-to-children relationship (British "disengaged" father).

Disengaged fathers also saw "visiting" as harmful to their children, especially in situations of extreme conflict between the spouses after divorce—adding to their feelings of hopelessness, resignation, and depression:

> It's no good at all—it affects them badly in all areas of their life. In a visiting relationship the children always get what they demand from the father, because the father will do anything he can so that the children enjoy themselves, just because he's not sure if he'll actually see them the next time. And when they go home the atmosphere with the mother is different, and they miss their father. It affects them at school, at home, and in their relationships with other children. They keep asking themselves why they don't see their father like they did before (Canadian "disengaged" father).

Those fathers who were highly involved with and attached to their children before divorce and managed to remain in contact with their children after divorce were those who were able to arrange (in most cases, mutually with their former spouses) an open and frequent schedule of contact with their children. These fathers reported that a cooperative and supportive post-divorce relationship had developed between the former spouses with regard to their parenting responsibilities. The nature of the non-custodial parent-child relationship is thus affected both by the frequency and length of contact after divorce, with frequent and lengthy contact (as opposed to "visiting") being much more likely to ensure continuity of contact in the case of fathers who were actively involved in their children's lives before divorce.

Perceived Effects of Divorce on Children

A primary factor associated with the disengagement of previously highly involved and attached fathers was their perception that their children were being "caught in the middle" of an adversarial legal process and an ongoing conflict between their parents. These fathers were reluctant to continue to expose their children to conflict or to utilize what they considered to be "violent" means to "win" their children's custody, a process they believed to be potentially highly damaging to their children. Fathers' prevailing concern for their children's well-being thus functioned as a "catch-22" against them: if a father was concerned about exposing his children to what he considered to be a "violent" process, or if he wished to not disrupt his children's lives further by challenging custody and upsetting their "status quo," his contact with his children after divorce may well have been in jeopardy.

Disengaged fathers were more attuned to the potentially negative impact of the divorce on their children, a reflection of their previous attachment to them. They believed that their children recognized their fathers' importance in their lives and would be severely affected by the rupture in the relationship. These fathers felt that their children's health and development was very much in jeopardy as a result of father absence after divorce:

> Given the close relationship that we had, I knew it would affect her negatively. I knew it would affect her, but in what way I didn't know. And I suppose I didn't give it the concern it should have received, in retrospect, because I thought it would only be a temporary situation. I suppose that this is how I've rationalized it (Canadian "disengaged" father).

> I don't feel that they've got a stable life, where they've got someone to fall back on to talk to. I know they've got their mother, but she's with them day after day, and it's not a shared responsibility. She just can't spend the time they need with them, whereas with two parents, you give each other a break, or you bring a different attitude toward them. They've only got one view of life, basically, and they don't have two people to give them a variation (British "disengaged" father).

I think they have lost a sense of security, and there is a total lack of any fatherly role, which I think is very detrimental to them. They've lost the love of and for their father (Canadian "disengaged" father).

He's very upset, sad, wondering why I've left, why his life has been turned upside-down. I'm very concerned about the long-term psychological effects—having a chip on his shoulder, wondering why his father left him (British "disengaged" father).

Paradoxically, disengaged fathers stressed the importance of continued paternal contact as critical to their children's well-being after divorce:

It is important to maintain the relationship in spite of the difficulties. It depends on the situation before separation. If the father had very little contact before separation, it's not so important to maintain links. But if he's closely involved in bringing up the child, he has to keep up the relationship. When it comes down to it, a person's security is rooted in his parents. This is very fundamental—security. A child should know where he came from, what his roots are (British "disengaged" father).

The effects on the father are double-edged. A little bit of contact for someone who wishes to be a full-time father is a crumb from the rich man's table, and I would feel that the little bit of contact would add greatly to the father's distress when he goes away, or when the child goes away. But that father is an adult and I think that disadvantage emotionally of the recurrent sore of leaving his own child has to be taken for the sake of that child (British "disengaged" father).

Cross-National Comparison

A final comment in regard to the data concerns the absence of findings of significant differences between the Canadian and British subsamples. Though some differences between fathers from Canada and Britain obtained in relation to some of the legal aspects of the divorce, these were negligible in comparison to the striking differences between contact and disengaged fathers in relation to a large number of variables. The differences between contact and disengaged fathers were virtually identical in the two locales. Where significant differences between fathers who remained in contact with and those who became disengaged from their children are reported, they applied equally to the Canadian and British subsamples.

Though in the Canadian context there appears to be wider public discussion of alternative post-divorce structural arrangements than in Britain, particularly in light of the higher rate of mothers with dependent children being employed on a full-time basis, legal structures and processes dominate in matters of child custody and access in both locales, and the actual outcomes of these processes are almost equivalent, with the percentage of divorced fathers who become non-custodial parents and the influence of the legal system in promoting traditional family structures after divorce being the same. The legal appropriation of custody and access determination—and the consequences of this—are similar in the two jurisdictions.

The main findings of the study—the grief reaction of non-custodial fathers attendant to divorce, the discontinuity between pre- and post-divorce father-child relationships, the discrepancy between fathers' stated desires during divorce and what they finally obtain through the legal system—were equally manifest in Canada and Britain. The lack of any substantive differences in the geographical comparison, with parallel data obtaining between Canada and Britain, limits alternative hypotheses, contributes to the validity of the data, and allows a measure of generalizability of the findings not otherwise available.

6

Practice and Policy Implications

The results of this study have ramifications for clinical practice with fathers and families and for family policy formulation in Canada and beyond. The division between therapeutic and policy implications is a loose one: the two are interrelated and in many instances overlap. They are thus presented as a "package" and are not meant to be received in isolation.

Custody and Access Alternatives

The findings of this study regarding the impact of divorce on non-custodial fathers complement existing studies that detail the chronic emotional and economic overload of custodial mothers solely responsible for their children after divorce, and the negative effects of the consequences of divorce on children's development and emotional well-being. They also support more recent divorce research suggesting that it is not divorce per se that results in the difficulties experienced by family members after divorce; rather, certain critical mediating factors stand between the event of divorce and post-divorce outcome for family members. These include the extent to which parents and children are able to maintain ongoing meaningful relationships, the level to which parents are able to support each other in their continuing parental roles, and the extent to which informal social networks and formal judicial, educational, and welfare institutions are supportive to a positive outcome in relation to these factors.

The disengagement of non-custodial fathers from the lives of their children after divorce, particularly those most involved with and attached to their children within the marriage, is largely the result of a custodial arrangement that they perceive as "disqualifying" them as parents. These fathers find that meaningful, regular, and frequent parenting is not possible within the bounds of sole maternal custody and limited paternal access. The very concept of "access" connotes for many fathers a de facto cessation of their parenting role. A significant number of fathers want to share in the parenting of their children after divorce, an arrangement by which they can retain a semblance of "real fatherhood," as opposed to the avuncular nature of the "visiting" relationship.

Many of the disengaged fathers in the sample suggested that a shared parenting arrangement would have allowed them to continue their previous parenting role. If indeed the most vulnerable group of fathers who lose post-divorce contact with their children are those who were previously most actively involved with and attached to their children, and if we accept research evidence that the key factor in the positive outcome of most children after divorce is the continued involvement of both parents in child rearing (Wallerstein and Kelly 1980; Hetherington et al. 1978; Hess and Camara 1979), the appropriateness of sole custody determinations is called into question, and the desirability of shared parenting as an alternative arrangement warrants serious consideration. In cases where both parents possess adequate parenting abilities, have been salient individuals in their children's lives, and wish to maintain their parenting responsibilities in an active manner following divorce, this kind of arrangement may potentially have the most positive long-term benefits for all family members.

Alternative Child Custody Options

The great majority of legal custody determinations, contested and uncontested, have taken the form of maternal custody with paternal access provisions. However, in recent years, novel custodial arrangements have evolved outside the judicial system as alternatives to traditional arrangements, and these have been instituted in the main by families themselves. These include various forms of shared parenting or "joint custody." In fact, considerable disagreement is found related to the definition of joint custody and the appropriate time arrangement it requires. In some instances, the distinguishing feature of joint custody is seen to be allowing both parents to retain *legal* responsibility and authority for major decisions affecting children. In other instances, joint custody is defined as an arrangement where both parents retain not only legal but also *physical* custody and they jointly and roughly equally provide for the day-to-day care of their children. Thus, joint custody may mean that both parents have legal custody, with one parent being the primary physical custodian, or it may refer to a sharing of both legal and physical custody.

An important concern of some divorce scholars is that joint legal custody may empower fathers, allowing them control over their children (and ex-wives) without any demonstration of responsibility for child care on their part (Fineman 1988; Weitzman 1985). Where joint custody dispositions continue to resemble de facto sole maternal custody, the social role and functions of custodial mothers are maintained in practice, but their legal rights and control over their children's lives are largely removed. Although joint legal custody has been shown to permit and facilitate joint physical custody, the potential for abuse and inequity remains in those cases where parental rights are granted via joint legal custody without any corresponding requirement for the assumption of active responsibility for child care.

The term "shared parenting," however, refers to a post-divorce parenting arrangement that attempts to approximate the parent-child relationships in the original two-parent home, in which both parents have not only equal rights and responsibilities for their children's welfare and upbringing but have an active role to play in the daily routines of their children's care and development, and in which both remain salient attachment figures in their children's lives. As the living arrangement that most closely resembles the pre-divorce family in cases where both parents had an active parenting role before divorce, shared parenting encompasses both shared physical caretaking (the actual day-to-day care of children) and equal authority regarding children's education, medical care, and religious upbringing.

The therapeutic community has generally viewed shared parenting in a favourable light, as the living arrangement that most closely resembles the pre-divorce family in the majority of cases and as an arrangement that fits best with emerging models of marriage and parenthood—with the notable exception of Goldstein et al. (1973) who argued for a legal presumption of sole custody based on the assumption of children having one "psychological parent" with whom they maintain a continuous, day-to-day relationship and constant bond. According to their formulation, a continuous relationship with the custodial parent is necessary for the child's healthy development, which may be disrupted by a continued relationship with the non-custodial parent: "The non-custodial parent should have no legally enforceable right to visit the child and the custodial (or "psychological") parent should have the right to decide whether it is desirable for the child to visit." This position, however, lacking any substantiating empirical data, has been vigorously challenged by more recent empirical evidence demonstrating that children form salient attachments to both parents, and that a continuous and meaningful post-divorce relationship with both parents, along with a reduction or cessation of interparental conflict, are critical mediating factors that can contribute to positive post-divorce outcome. In this context, it has been suggested that shared parenting may be the most desirable custody disposition for the majority of all family members (Bowman and Ahrons, 1985; Irving et al. 1984; Folberg 1984).

Shared Parenting as an Alternative to Sole Custody

In sole custody, courts give to one parent the rights and responsibilities for a child's care and control that had previously been held by the two parents together: divorce is understood to require that one parent relinquish care and control over the child, as the custodial parent effectively assumes full authority. Legal sole custody awards represent a public acknowledgement and notice that the role of the non-custodial parent is expected to be substantially reduced (Richards 1982). In its pattern of awarding sole maternal custody in both contested and uncontested cases, the judicial system legitimates and strengthens "traditional" family norms and gender-based structural inequities: a mother's post-divorce role is assumed to be synonymous with full-time parenthood and the father's with economic provision. Such custody determinations effectively "disqualify" previously involved fathers as active parents, leave mothers with the sole responsibility for their children, and result in children being deprived of a salient attachment figure in their lives.

There is a relative paucity of research on alternative child custody options, but a number of recent studies have supported shared parenting or joint physical custody as a viable and optimal structural arrangement for many families after divorce. Ahrons (1980) discovered that "joint custody" applies to a wide variety of parenting arrangements and relationships among families. She found that not all joint custody parents are amicable, nor do they always share responsibility equally for their children. The amount of interparental support and conflict was found to be a strong predictor of shared parental responsibility and decision-making, but it was not a significant predictor of the amount of time fathers spent with their children or their involvement in activities with them. Regardless of whether joint custody parents supported each other or were in conflict, joint custody fathers were significantly more involved in post-divorce parenting than non-custodial fathers.

Leupnitz (1982) interviewed children as well as parents and compared sole maternal, sole paternal, and shared parenting structures, concluding that children are more satisfied with shared rather than with sole parenting arrangements. Shiller (1984) found that divorce causes less trauma and dislocation to children whose parents opt for shared parenting and that these children in shared parenting families appear to be more comfortable with the status quo, with a more realistic image of what the future will bring. Wolchik et al. (1985) discovered that children in shared parenting homes report a significantly higher number of positive experiences than children in sole parenting arrangements. Lund (1987) compared children and parents in "single-parent/father absent" families with those in "conflicted co-parenting" and "harmonious co-parenting" families and, utilizing independent teacher ratings and using interviews with parents and their children, concluded that children are functioning best in harmonious co-parenting families and least in single-parent families.

Irving et al. (1984) studied shared parenting, utilizing a large data base and following families for a comparatively longer period of time than previous research. Contrary to expectations, they found that shared parenting is a realistic consideration for all economic groups, an idea that was obscured by the preponderance of middle- and upper-class families reported in earlier studies. Also, parents with initial doubts and some reluctance about opting for co-parenting were able to negotiate shared parenting plans and reported positive long-term outcomes. It was not necessary for co-parents to be favourably disposed to each other for the arrangement to work—although most respondents reported a change in their feelings towards their former spouses, typically becoming more positive—nor was it necessary for parents to have had a high level of cooperation in sharing parental responsibilities during the marriage. In almost all cases, the initial consideration of the possibility of a shared parenting relationship was first raised by one of the parents rather than by lawyers, mediators, family therapists, or other professionals. Overall, nearly 90 percent of co-parents were in favour of the arrangement. The authors concluded that shared parenting is a viable option for a range of divorcing couples, but not for everyone. Good predictors of outcome success include a commitment to parenting, reasonable communication skills, flexibility, the ability to separate previous marital conflicts from matters concerning the children, and good faith with regard to agreements made. Conversely, intense and continuing conflict, weak commitment to active parenting, and irrational hope of reconciliation were all predictors of outcome failure.

An important caveat must be made in interpreting the results of studies of shared parenting because most involve parents who have selected such arrangements themselves. Brotsky et al. (1988), however, reported on a study of a pilot mediation service designed to promote shared parenting in cases where at least one of the parties was opposed to the arrangement, in a jurisdiction where mandatory mediation is intended to promote shared parenting. When educated about children's needs in divorce and informed of the range of parenting options open to them, 80 percent of participants opted for a shared parenting arrangement. In a one-year follow-up of these mediated arrangements, the authors found that shared parenting provided stability (93 percent of cases), parental satisfaction (68 percent), valuing of the other spouse (97 percent), and comfort for the children in relation to both parents (82 percent). When compared with those in sole parenting arrangements, children in shared parenting homes, like their parents, were reported to be functioning better in all areas.

In sum, proponents of shared parenting have stated their "case" from both the perspective of the children and each of the parents. The central hazard that divorce poses to a child's emotional health and development is the diminished or disrupted parenting that occurs during and after divorce (Wallerstein and Kelly 1980; Mitchell 1985). Shared parenting spares children the disruption and feeling of rejection following the departure of one parent. It ensures the preservation of attachment bonds with both parents in a continuous, secure, and protected relationship. Because shared parenting enables each parent to rest and enjoy periods of solitude, the resultant lower level of stress can contribute to parents' increased emotional availability to their children (Folberg and Graham 1981). Shared parenting exposes children to two lifestyles and two points of view, offering a larger array of positive characteristics to model and a greater variety of cognitive and social stimulation. In providing for active parenting by two nurturing figures, shared parenting may contribute to a breakdown of gender-differentiated character structures in children (Folberg and Graham 1981; Richards 1982).

Many sole custodial mothers feel that their children overburden and imprison them, and there is strong evidence that these mothers become physically and emotionally exhausted, as well as socially isolated (Wallerstein and Kelly 1980; Folberg and Graham 1981). Thus, in a study of divorced parents who shared parenting, mothers reported that the greatest advantage of the arrangement was the sharing of responsibility for their children (Nehls and Morgenbesser 1980). Non-custodial fathers feel themselves to be "disqualified" as active caretakers, but shared parenting fathers report that the greatest advantage of sharing care is the opportunity to maintain an active and meaningful role in their children's lives in "normal" day-to-day living situations. Those fathers previously highly involved and attached to their children are able to continue to be centrally responsible for and involved in their care and development and are afforded the daily intimate contact that living together, rather than "visiting," provides. Those fathers previously on the periphery of their children's lives are presented, if they so desire, with a unique opportunity to become competent, caring, and nurturant parents and to enhance their relationship with their children.

Research studies have provided substantial empirical support for shared parenting as a viable post-divorce option for families, from both the perspective of children and the entire family system, but a number of concerns have been expressed among legal scholars in particular with regard to various aspects of such arrangements. Some legal researchers (Fineman 1988; Polikoff 1982) have argued in favour of a sole custody "primary caretaker" presumption as preferable to shared parenting, questioning the degree to which shared parenting actually reflects pre-divorce family structures. These writers have rightly cautioned against uncritical acceptance of the position that women and men make undifferentiated, exchangeable contributions to parenting during the marriage. It may be questioned, however, whether sole custody is in fact more reflective of pre-divorce family structures than shared parenting. Though mothers generally assume the major responsibility for child care before divorce, in the majority of cases both parents form close and unique personal bonds with their children and remain uniquely influential in their development (Lewis 1986; Lamb 1986; Parke 1981). This is reflected after divorce in children's pervasive longing for their non-custodial parent. The primary caretaker presumption fails to make the distinction between involvement, attachment, and influence of parents, nor (like the "one psychological parent" position of Goldstein et al. [1973]) does it recognize the existence of a heterogeneity of parenting roles in families, including shared parenting arrangements before divorce (Ehrensaft 1980).

An issue of considerable debate regarding shared parenting is the ex-spouses' ability to cooperate: shared parenting can be calamitous if parents are unwilling or unable to cooperate, which some maintain is the case in the majority of divorces involving children. Folberg and Graham (1981), however, argue that the adversarial nature of the legal system, when extended to the issue of child custody, perpetuates a climate of animosity between persons who have already proven that they cannot get along together. To the extent that the legal system casts divorcing parents in the role of enemies and expects them to be unable to cooperate, a self-fulfilling prophecy is created. Our study suggests that legal processes not only exacerbate parental conflict, but they often create an atmosphere of hostility in cases where relatively amicable negotiation may have taken place.

Although it has been frequently suggested that shared parenting can work only for couples with an amicable relationship, the pertinent question should be whether divorced parents are able to isolate their marital conflicts from their roles as parents. There is strong empirical evidence that a divorced couple that makes a commitment to share the care of their children is able to cooperate even though they continue to feel considerable antagonism towards each other—what often begins as a "front," an appearance of minimal conflict in the children's presence, becomes in time a "normal" pattern of relating, a self-fulfilling prophecy (Irving et al. 1984). When neither parent feels threatened with the possibility of loss, each is in a healthier position for cooperation (Calvin 1981). Also, as mentioned, shared parenting allows a combination of "time off" and enhanced involvement in child care, overcoming the problems of mothers who may feel overwhelmed by sole responsibility for children and of fathers who feel excluded from their children's lives.

Another major concern about shared parenting is that it may be disruptive and confusing for children to have two homes, where they encounter two different lifestyles and value systems. It is argued that shared parenting inherently creates an unstable, impermanent condition for children. A child in a shared parenting situation will be "bounced" from parent to parent and his or her loyalties will be divided; therefore, "stability" and "continuity" require that custody be held by only one parent (Goldstein et al. 1973). In rebuttal, it has been emphasized that children have strong attachment bonds and relationships with both parents and show remarkable tenacity in continuing these under a variety of conditions (Richards 1982).

A number of studies have sought to weigh the advantages for children of having two "psychological parents" after divorce against the problems created by two separate residences, to determine whether living in two homes undermines stability. Greif (1979) concluded that the concern over the disruption of having two homes is rarely a concern of members of shared parenting families themselves. Abarbanel (1979) observed shared custody families in California and found that children feel "at home" in both environments and see themselves as living in two homes. She concluded that the children of the families studied did in fact have "two psychological parents, not one." Others have argued that sole custody deprives children of being exposed to another world view from the non-custodial parent which would better equip them for life in a pluralistic society. Sole custody can sever a child's ties with an entire set of relatives, but shared parenting allows the child's support group to expand to include not only both parents and their relatives but also each parent's new friends. Thus, whereas Goldstein et al. (1973) emphasize the child's vulnerability and need for a consistent and predictable world, their critics emphasize the child's resilience and need for emotional support and stimulation from diverse sources.

It is now generally recognized that a child's "best interests" are interdependent with and to a large extent a by-product of the "best interests" of their parents (Folberg and Graham 1981). A new concept of the post-divorce family is emerging that views divorce not as *dissolving* the family but as a crisis in the family life cycle that requires a *rearrangement* of family relationships (Ahrons 1980). Elkin (1978) observes that "the very decision of divorce may be a family's way of trying to salvage the family by putting the pieces together in different ways." Of the many possible family patterns that can emerge after divorce, one is the establishment of separate maternal and paternal households still connected by the attachment bonds of the parents to the children and the children to the parents—an arrangement where both parents retain "custody" of their children.

The potential of shared parenting to be an alternative to traditional custody and access arrangements is supported by the present study. The following are offered as recommendations for the consideration of shared parenting as an alternative to traditional custody and access arrangements.

1. Redefining joint custody as shared parenting. The term, "joint custody" has assumed a variety of meanings in the literature, referring to a plethora of custodial arrangements where both parents participate in their children's lives after divorce. Joint custody may mean that both parents simultaneously have legal custody, with one parent being the primary physical custodian, or it may refer to a sharing of both legal and physical custody.

As discussed earlier, an important concern of some divorce scholars is that joint legal custody may empower fathers, allowing them control over their children (and ex-wives) without any demonstration of responsibility for child care on their part (Fineman 1988; Weitzman 1985). The degree to which legal joint custody reflects de facto post-divorce family structures strikes at the heart of the joint custody debate. Where joint custody dispositions continue to resemble de facto sole maternal custody, the social role and functions of custodial mothers are maintained in practice, but their legal rights and control over their children's lives are largely removed. From children's point of view, such "joint custody" is likely to be meaningless. Though joint legal custody has been shown to permit and facilitate joint physical custody—the evidence cited above indicates that de jure joint custody fathers are in fact significantly more involved in de facto parenting than non-custodial fathers—the potential for abuse and inequity remains in those cases where parental rights are granted via joint legal custody without any corresponding requirement for the assumption of active responsibility for child care.

"Custody" of children should involve both physical custody—the actual day-to-day caretaking of children—and legal custody—arrangements regarding children's education, medical care, religious upbringing, and so on. "Shared parenting" captures both elements. The assumption of parental rights without concomitant expectations regarding shared post-divorce child-care participation has the potential for serious abuse. If, in joint custody, parenting is not de facto a shared activity, and if mothers remain as primary caretakers of children, then it may well be argued that "the search for symbolic equality has led to a sacrifice of equity" (Fineman 1988). Shared parenting requires a sharing of both elements by each parent. This does not necessarily mean a precise apportioning of a child's time on an equal or "fifty-fifty" basis, as flexibility based on children's and parents' needs is important, but the concept should include the notion of two actively involved parents having regular and frequent physical contact and caring for their children within a daily routine in separate households.

2. Sanctioning shared parenting. The findings of this study support the ideal of shared parenting and the social sanction for such an arrangement. Instead of legal joint custody orders, the preservation of existing bonds and relationships in the form of a presumption of shared parenting after divorce may be a more appropriate symbol of continuing parent-child relationships and their immunity to the termination of the marital relationship. According to Burgoyne et al. (1987:40):

> Within marriage, custody is held jointly and equally by both parents and it is necessary to question whether that situation should be changed by divorce. Indeed, this could be put more positively; at the end of a marriage it might be desirable to reaffirm the role of both parents and so make it clear that although the divorce is the end of the parents' marital relationship, their parental rights—to use an old-fashioned term—and duties persist. One way to symbolize the two partners' continuing roles is to have a joint custody order or, as some have suggested, to make no order at all about custody so that the situation that obtained in the marriage persists.

In no way should shared parenting be coerced in cases where both parents desire a sole custody arrangement or demonstrate a weak commitment to shared parenting. Further, there are clear contraindications to shared parenting (and often parental access), such as spousal and child abuse, child neglect or exploitation, the physical or psychological incapacity of a parent, chronic alcoholism or drug addiction, or a stated disinterest in caring for the children. If a child indicates fear of one parent's unpredictability or abuse, or consistently refuses to spend time with that parent, the desirability of shared parenting must be called into question. The presumption of shared parenting is based upon the assumption that, in the majority of cases, both parents are capable, trustworthy, and loving custodians, but this presumption presupposes the need to differentiate carefully between those for whom shared parenting is an appropriate custody option and those for whom it is contraindicated. It can be argued that shared parenting is not in children's best interests in abusive relationships because of the overlap between child and spousal abuse, and because the assaultive male may gain more potential opportunities to continue his domination and control over the former spouse and children (Pagelow 1990). Factors related to negative outcomes in shared parenting include extreme hostility and anger, a need to punish the former partner, projection of blame, low self-esteem, and extreme rigidity (Brotsky et al. 1988; Johnston and Campbell 1988).

3. Therapeutic support for shared parenting. The obstacles to shared parenting are numerous, as are the challenges that face the divorced family. Shared parenting requires an extremely high level of organization, cooperation, and commitment, at a time when emotional resources are likely to be extremely low. Shared parenting is an arrangement that deviates from the norm, and co-parents are likely to feel like pioneers. Each shared parenting arrangement must be tailor-made to the specific family.

With adequate therapeutic support, however, the ideal of shared parenting could become a reality for a significant proportion of divorced families. Therapeutic support can help to diffuse situations of high conflict (which warrant against the adoption of a shared parenting arrangement), can introduce the option of shared parenting to divorcing parents, and can help them to create conditions conducive to the success of such an arrangement. In shared parenting counselling, attention is focused not on past-oriented marital and affective issues, but on present and future parental issues of a rational and cognitive nature.

An agreeable and workable shared parenting plan is the ultimate aim of shared parenting counselling. Initially, such counselling is seen as highly educative, involving the sharing of information about children's developmental needs and their need for the active post-divorce involvement of both parents. The feasibility of a shared parenting arrangement could then be examined from the parents' perspective, with each parent being asked to outline their parenting needs and interests (indicating the amount of time they would like to invest) and to evaluate their own parenting strengths and weaknesses. Factors of geography, number and ages of children, and children's school and peer involvement can then be examined, as well as the practical needs and constraints of day-to-day concerns and the realities of the entire family. A range of daily, weekly, and monthly schedules could then be considered: alternatives include sharing children on a daily basis, such as with one parent during the daytime and with the other in the evenings; a split week, with one parent three days per week and with the other four days, alternating every other week or month; and alternating weeks, every two weeks, three weeks, one month, and so on. With young children, who have a limited sense of time, it may be desirable to see both parents on a relatively frequent basis; parents should be urged to maintain residences in the same geographical locale at least until their children get older. The latter arrangement may be optimal for children of all ages, allowing them to stay in the same school and neighbourhood, to play with the same friends, and to be with both parents on a regular and frequent basis.

The final stage of shared parenting counselling is plan formulation, moving from a skeletal structure to the specifics of the shared parenting arrangement. As much specificity as possible may be required initially to avoid future confusion and conflict, including details of scheduling contact with the children, and a listing of which responsibilities are shared and which are held by each parent. Parents can be assisted in identifying those issues that require joint consensus and consultation (such as child management and discipline strategies, medical care, education, and religious training) and aided in their negotiation of these. Over time, flexibility should be encouraged; contingencies are needed as unexpected events can and do occur. Parents should be prepared to react with consideration and resilience rather than with rigidity and to stick to the "spirit" of the plan rather than to the "letter." Other issues, potential obstacles, and areas of conflict regarding parenting can then be examined to help parents to develop workable methods for dealing with them as they occur. In addition, issues of possible remarriage, geographical relocation, and how to deal with children's changing developmental needs should be considered. Finally, parents should be urged to return for theraputic support as future issues develop.

Custody and Access Determination

The majority of fathers in the present study described the legal system as exacerbating or creating conflict between the former spouses, setting a tone for the post-divorce relationship that did not bode well for fathers' future contact with their children. They felt that a more "conciliatory" approach that brought both parents together to negotiate custody and access arrangements would have produced more beneficial results for themselves and their children.

Their views complement current research on the impact of divorce on children. A critical variable affecting the adjustment of children after divorce is the extent of continued involvement by both parents in child rearing and divorces having the least detrimental effect on the development of children are those in which the parents are able to cooperate in their continuing parental roles (Wallerstein and Kelly 1980; Hetherington et al. 1978; Hess and Camara, 1979). If parental cooperation can be freed from the marital tension that may have adversely affected the children within the marriage, then the divorce may present a positive developmental influence. Rarely, however, is this an outcome of a legal mode of custody and access determination.

If indeed the legal system exacerbates or creates conflict between the spouses after divorce, contributing to fathers' disengagement from their children, and if we accept research findings that stress the importance of parental cooperation after divorce for children's ongoing development and emotional well-being, then the disadvantages of legal determination of child custody and access and the need for alternative mechanisms are clear. Mediation and related counselling services could provide an effective alternative to a legal and judicial means of resolving issues of child custody and access for the majority of divorcing families.

Alternatives to the Adversarial Approach

The many difficulties inherent in an adversarial approach to custody and access resolution, combined with accumulated research data showing that a cessation of interparental conflict is critical to children's post-divorce adjustment, has led many to conclude that the legal process is a largely unsatisfactory means of determining post-divorce arrangements for children. Of the existing mechanisms of dispute resolution—adjudication, arbitration, mediation and negotiation— mediation has been identified as the most appropriate alternative to litigation in family and custody disputes.

Mediation has been defined as "a process of resolving disputes in which a neutral third party assists the disputing parties to reach a mutually acceptable solution" (McWhinney 1988); Irving, Benjamin, et al. (1981:42) see mediation in divorce to be

> a form of family intervention involving both spouses seen together and designed to achieve one or more of the following outcomes: reduce the level of real or perceived conflict between spouses; facilitate communication between spouses, either in general terms or about specific issues problematic for them; transform an amorphous problem into a resolvable issue; suggest problem-solving strategies as a viable alternative to litigation; provide the most efficient use of the legal system; and optimally help the spouses achieve a written agreement concerning one or more disputable issues or problems.

To accomplish these goals, the process of mediation is usually highly structured, setting the context for negotiation and proceeding through identifiable stages, from gathering information to reaching and drafting an agreement. The main strategies of mediation include those designed to elicit cooperation between the parents, as well as skills and techniques for managing conflict (Saposnek 1982). Parkinson (1987) identifies the main tasks of mediation as simultaneously engaging both partners to work on a mutually agreed agenda as early as possible in the course of separation; providing space and structure; redefining roles within the family, in particular separating the parenting from spousal roles; and using a pragmatic, short-term, task-centred problem-solving approach towards custody and access disputes.

The growing literature on mediation has highlighted a number of its benefits over litigation. Kressel (1987) identifies a better opportunity for the parties' needs to emerge and be accommodated during negotiations; an increase in their sense of competence, self-determination and mastery; the development of problem-solving skills in dealing with one another which will be of value during the post-divorce period; the creation of a greater sense of "ownership" of the agreement and hence an increased probability of adherence to it; and an appreciable reduction in legal fees. Smith (1981) stresses that parents are usually open to changes in their behaviour towards their children and each other, and that mediation can use this willingness to diffuse anger and resolve underlying emotional issues. Mnookin and Kornhauser (1979) outline the benefits of mediation for children: parents are more knowledgeable about a child's needs, desires, and circumstances than a lawyer or judge, and mediation is more likely to result in ongoing post-divorce relationships between children and both of their parents.

Mediation as an Alternative to Litigation

There is substantial evidence of a strong link between mediation and positive post-divorce relationships between both parents and their children. Child custody and access resolution by means of mediation is associated with a more cooperative attitude between parents, more regular contact between both parents and their children, and greater compliance with terms of negotiated agreements, including financial arrangements made outside the arena of mediation (Parkinson 1987; Ogus et al. 1989; Brotsky et al. 1988; Pearson and Thoennes 1984; Irving, Benjamin, et al. 1981). By educating parents in the management of conflict and teaching them to communicate directly about their ongoing parental responsibilities, and by focusing on the parenting qualities and potentialities of each partner rather than on previous marital discord, mediation can set a tone conducive to a relatively harmonious post-divorce parental relationship. By providing an opportunity for each parent's needs to emerge and be accommodated during negotiations, it can facilitate the active involvement of both parents with their children after divorce.

The effectiveness of mediation as an interventive strategy, either alone or in comparison to litigation, is empirically supported. The Toronto Conciliation Project (Irving, Benjamin, et al. 1981), a longitudinal study that used a comparative research design and a random sample of divorcing couples, began in 1976. The results of this study indicate a number of major benefits of mediation over litigation: a substantial majority (70 percent) of parents successfully reached agreement in matters of custody, access, and support; agreements reached through mediation tended to endure (less than 10 percent returned to court at the one-year follow-up); parents consistently reported that mediation reduced conflict and emotional tension while facilitating better communication and mutual understanding; by its combination of objective outcome (agreement) and subjective relief, mediation was strongly associated with significant improvements in life circumstances and assured regular access and that support payments were made; and mediation proved to be a cost-effective method of post-divorce dispute resolution. The findings of Irving and his associates have been corroborated by a number of North American studies; mandatory mediation has been introduced in several U.S. jurisdictions, providing researchers with a unique opportunity to examine its effectiveness (Brotsky et al. 1988; Kressel 1987; Sprenkle and Storm 1983). In surveys of British mediation services, agreement rates of over 75 percent have been consistently reported (Forster 1982; Parkinson 1986); again, agreements made during the course of mediation were seen as durable in the majority of cases, and a strong correlation was noted between early contact and outcome. The Conciliation Project Unit (Ogus et al. 1989), examined the effectiveness of mediation in Britain and distinguished settlement rate (and the durability of settlement), improvement of communication between the parties and reduction of conflict, change in participants' psychological well-being, and consumer satisfaction. They found that although mediation interventions were highly variable, with differences in emphasis, length, and mediators' styles, users of mediation services reported agreement on at least some of the issues dealt with in mediation in 71 percent of cases, and 74 percent of these parties described themselves as satisfied with the agreements reached. A number of factors were found to be critical to the various dimensions of mediation effectiveness, including the difficulty of the case, the range of issues undertaken, the content and location of mediation, and whether or not other divorce-related issues were being dealt with by means of lawyer negotiation or litigation.

Most studies of mediation outcome have tended to overlook the fact that family mediation is far from a monolithic process, because a number of practice models have been developed and are in use. There are wide variations in the structure, staffing, and working methods of mediation. McWhinney (1988) has identified three main vehicles for the delivery of mediation services in Canada: the court system, the private sector, and social service agencies. Although the number of mediation services is growing, many questions remain to be resolved. There has been considerable debate in relation to a number of practice issues: What types of services are best suited to family and divorce-related issues? Mediation services can be court-based or independent, with distinct advantages and disadvantages in each case. The issues of confidentiality and privilege have provoked considerable discussion. Should mediation be open or closed? Who should be the mediators, and what practice standards and training criteria should guide their work? Which divorce-related issues are best dealt with by mediation, and which by more traditional legal approaches? Should the financial aspects of division of property and support payments be included in mediation or left within the legal arena? Is mediation more cost-effective than litigation, and what forms of public and/or private funding should obtain? Mediation can be voluntary or involuntary, and the issue of mandatory mediation is contentious. What are the specific contraindications to mediation? Should mediators adopt a neutralist or interventive role? While some theorists espouse an educative function for the mediator, others take a more limited focus and view mediation strictly as a means to resolve disputes between couples regarding custody and access. Should mediation be therapeutically oriented or structured strictly towards settling disputes? The involvement of children and significant others in the process of mediation represents another area of disagreement among practitioners, as does the participation of lawyers. Concern has been expressed that mediation reinforces unequal power relationships between the parties, where women in particular may be at a disadvantage. Finally, the field of mediation derives most of its concepts and terminology from the disciplines of law and social work, creating considerable confusion. The differences between mediation and reconciliation, mediation and marital or family counselling, and mediation and divorce counselling are often unclear.

While these ideological debates and variations in practice continue, an increasing number of empirical investigations are beginning to clarify some of the essential questions related to family mediation. Findings from these and from studies on the impact of divorce on children and parents may be compared to the data contained herein. The following, based upon key findings in current divorce-related research and the data from this study, are offered as key recommendations regarding mediation as an alternative to litigation:

1. **Diagnostic, educative and advocacy focus of mediation.** In recognition of the fact that the positive post-divorce adjustment of children is associated with ongoing meaningful contact with both parents, and that, from children's perspective, traditional sole custody arrangements with limited access to the non-custodial parent are woefully inadequate, a basic assumption of mediation should be that termination of a marriage necessitates a restructuring of family life that enables children to have a meaningful and active relationship with both parents. In light of the fact that more than 50 percent of non-custodial fathers disengage from their children's lives after divorce—despite, as we have seen, these fathers' relatively high levels of involvement with and emotional attachment to their children during the marriage and their desire for at least partial physical custody after divorce—the supportive maintenance of the father-child relationship should be an important goal of mediation. Specifically, family mediation should facilitate the exploration of shared parenting as a viable custodial arrangement.

Most would agree that the mediator should have an implicit ethical responsibility to influence a settlement that is in the "most adequate" if not "best interests" of the child. At the time of divorce, particularly in the midst of feelings of anger, bitterness, and rejection, parents may be relatively insensitive to the needs and feelings of their children (Mitchell 1985; Wallerstein and Kelly 1980). In this regard, mediators with expertise in the expected effects of divorce on children can be instrumental in helping parents to recognize the psychological, social, and economic consequences of divorce on their children, to take measures to provide comfort and appropriate understanding, and, most critically, to make arrangements that proceed from the perspective of children's best interests in divorce. The quality of post-divorce parenting available to children should guide the process of mediation, not simply the need to reach agreement on disputed issues, and mediators should actively encourage parents to primarily consider the needs of their children in their negotiations over post-divorce living arrangements. Thorough assessments of the nature of pre-existing parent-child relationships, and the spousal relationship, are crucial.

Courts and lawyers rarely deviate from precedent (sole maternal custody with paternal access), but mediation should offer broader possibilities and expand the range of options for post-divorce parenting. Whether, in practice, mediation challenges or reinforces gender inequality is central to the mediation debate. Whereas the legal system reinforces prevailing structures of gender-based inequality, mediation may seek to challenge traditional arrangements. If mediation counselling does not exercise its educative and advocacy functions, by stressing the necessity of regular and frequent post-divorce contact by both parents with their children, by detailing the range of custody and access options open to families and, where appropriate, by actively facilitating and working through the logistics of a shared parenting arrangement, it fails to realize its true potential.

Current research examining the link between mediation and shared parenting corroborates the findings of the study. Koopman et al. (1984)—in a comparative analysis of mediated and non-mediated child custody and access arrangements, where the goal of mediation was to "restructure, not break" families and to provide for the continuing post-divorce parenting of both parents—found that in 88 percent of the cases where mediation was provided, parents chose the option of shared parenting. The investigators concluded that the maternal custody arrangements prevalent in the non-mediated arrangements (where *no* parents opted for shared parenting) are "likely to be the result of societal traditions and expectations, along with ignorance of the fact that parents have choices among a variety of potentially viable arrangements" (Koopman et al. 1984:23). They further found that when a comprehensive concern for the "best interests of the family" (referring to the quality, quantity, and consistency of children's contact with both parents) is incorporated into mediated agreements, the prognosis for compliance in all areas of child-related concerns—financial, educational, residential, medical, and relational—are enhanced (Koopman et al. 1984:24). Brotsky et al. (1988) and Zemmelman et al. (1987) reported on a longitudinal study in California of a mandatory mediation model designed to assist parents in resolving custody and access disputes, encouraging shared parenting where appropriate. In addition to mediation, the model combined group treatment, divorce counselling, child assessment, and play therapy/counselling. The end result was the development of a written parenting agreement, and the process focused mainly on children's needs and experiences (the child assessment steered the process towards a consideration of the "best interests of the child"), reduction of hostility, and providing a model for and practice in problem solving. The mediation process was thus highly therapeutic, and mediators also functioned as child advocates, guiding custody plans towards the specific needs of children. Results showed that of the fifty-one families in the project, thirty-eight couples developed some form of shared parenting agreement, ten failed to reach an agreement (eight of whom returned to court), and three reconciled during or after mediation. In a one-year follow-up, children and parents with shared parenting arrangements demonstrated an improved adaptation to divorce and functioned at a higher level in all areas, as opposed to those in other custodial arrangements (Brotsky et al. 1988). Thus mediation can be used effectively to reduce anxiety about shared parenting and promote agreement on post-divorce shared parenting arrangements.

In helping couples to draft custody and access agreements, the mediator has a unique opportunity to educate parents about the variety of options available and what impact these options will have on their own and their children's lives. Examining the feasibility of shared parenting arrangements in situations where both parents had developed attachment bonds with their children is likely to have a profound impact upon lowering the disengagement rates of fathers after divorce and to contribute to positive post-divorce outcomes for all members of the divorced family.

An assessment of pre-divorce spousal relationships, with a particular focus on power relationships between the couple, is also critical in the early stages of the mediation process. Power is rarely equal between couples, whereas mediation requires an equality of bargaining power. Mediation has the potential, however, to identify dynamics of power and control that might otherwise remain hidden, and thus ultimately can become a highly empowering process for the spouse with less power to express her or his interests in divorce. Initial screening in cases of spouse abuse aims towards the creation of an agreement that controls the level of contact between parents and ensures protection and safety. Mediation should also reinforce the criminal nature of violent behaviour and should be seen as an adjunct to legal and therapeutic processes in abuse cases. Mediation can educate battered women about their legal options, and legal consequences may be made explicit to assaultive men. Legal representation, protective restraining orders, or therapeutic services may be required as conditions for mediation to proceed (Girdner, 1990; Pagelow, 1990).

2. Therapeutic, longer-term focus of mediation. Greater attention should be placed on the durability of mediated agreements and the necessity for parents to increase their ability to cooperate and negotiate with each other in relation to their ongoing parental responsibilities. Once a parenting plan has been negotiated and drafted, it should be implemented for a specified trial period, with therapeutic support and troubleshooting during this time. The plan is then reviewed and made permanent, modified, or abandoned altogether. Knowing at the outset that a shared parenting arrangement will be reviewed formally after a specified trial period will help parents to agree to try the arrangement despite their anxiety about committing themselves to an unknown way of life—this can be a "safety valve" for parents.

The mediator's primary goal during this period is to assist the parents in the initial stages of the new shared parenting arrangement to facilitate their own and their children's adaptation to living as two households. Over time, the task of the mediator will be to move the parents from "parallel parenting" to cooperative shared parenting (Ricci 1980). Over time, flexibility, creativity, and compromise should be encouraged. Contingencies will be needed as unexpected events will occur. Again, parents should be prepared to react with consideration and resilience rather than with rigidity, to stick to the "spirit" of the plan rather than to the "letter."

A five-stage therapeutic/interventionist model of divorce mediation is proposed (Kruk, 1993):

1. Assessment: The needs and interests of the children and parents are evaluated; the nature of pre-existing parent-child bonds and the level of interspousal conflict are carefully examined to determine if mediation is appropriate and shared parenting is indicated for the post-divorce family,

2. Education: Children's needs and interests in divorce are considered in detail, with the aim of heightening the parents' understanding of the impact of divorce on their children and children's needs in the post-divorce period, family needs in divorce, and how the process of mediation will address those needs. Agreement is reached regarding the development of a parenting agreement that will consider the children's needs first and foremost,

3. Advocacy: Where indicated, the desirability of a shared parenting arrangement that meets the children's needs and the parents' is actively promoted,

4. Facilitation of negotiations: An individualized shared parenting plan that outlines specific living arrangements, schedules, roles, and responsibilities is jointly developed,

5. Continuing support: Follow-up and assistance are provided in the implementation of the shared parenting plan.

3.   Mandatory introduction to mediation. Our findings support the call for a mandatory introduction to mediation in *most* disputed cases of child custody and access, with referral made at the time of the initial court hearing. Mediation should become an integral part of court procedure in contested cases (although the service itself should not be court-based), and courts should adjourn such cases to allow mediation to take place. Some would argue that the voluntary nature of mediation is an essential characteristic of the process, but others have emphasized that the public needs exposure to mediation, that the outcome of mediation is voluntary even when the process is not, and that a mandatory intoductory session to mediation need not interfere with one's right of access to the legal process. Given strong research findings that conflict between parents is detrimental to children's well-being, an attempt to settle custody and access disputes amicably should be made. In U.S. jurisdictions where mediation is mandatory, the service acts largely as a diversion from the potentially destructive experience of litigation.

At present, Canada has no statutory service to which individuals can turn for professional advice in the realm of marriage and divorce. In calling for the establishment of a national mediation service in Britain, Ogus et al. (1989) recommend that "the mediation service would be one part of a network of local services, independent of the courts. . . . The function of this network—which would be called 'The Family Advisory, Counselling and Mediation Bureau'— would differ from that of existing independent mediation in three important ways. . . . It would transcend what is in practice the rather artificial boundary which currently exists between marriage guidance and mediation agencies and would, in consequence, cater for a range of relationship difficulties . . . the agency would be multi-purpose and provide advice, counselling (for individuals, couples, children and other family members) and mediation. . . . The agency would fulfil an important educative function by providing centres at which advice and information regarding marriage, divorce, children and the legal system were readily available" (Ogus et al. 1989:360).

The fathers in the study spoke at length about the desirability of mediation over litigation but had been largely unaware of the existence of such services at the time of the divorce. An agency that provides a range of marriage, family, and divorce-related services (education and practical information, and therapeutic services on an individual, family, and group basis), self-help facilities, therapist training, and a research component under one roof could become a community focal point for the delivery of direct services, the development of new methods of work and evaluation of existing approaches, and the dissemination of marriage, family, and divorce-related information. In the first stage of a family's contact with such a service, assessment interviews could be utilized to determine the mode of intervention most likely to be beneficial and to ascertain the family's desires in this area. The range of available programs would assure the needed flexibility as family members "worked through" the various stages of the divorce. Further, a community-based service would facilitate early intervention, as timing of mediation is crucial to its success: if such support is provided early in the divorce process, a spirit of friendship and cooperation is more likely to survive the divorce (Irving, Benjamin et al. 1981). It would also allow a measure of flexibility not available within in-court services: flexibility in number of sessions, the review of negotiated arrangements after a trial period, regular follow-ups as modifications of the agreement became necessary, and the use of other forms of post-divorce counselling.

Mediation may be inappropriate in some cases or unsuccessful in assisting certain parents to reach an agreement regarding post-divorce parenting. There are contraindications to mediation. In cases of physical or sexual child abuse or serious neglect, and situations where abused spouses are unable to contemplate negotiating with their former partner, the option of legal proceedings regarding child custody and access must be available. Though mediation has been shown to be effective with many abusive families, a procedure that permits courts to exclude such cases from mediation is needed. Mediation should be discontinued if spousal or child abuse occurs during mediation despite legal sanctions and participation in treatment, if the abuser violates established safety boundaries, if past abuse has rendered the victimized party unable to represent her interests, or if the mediator is unable to control the abuser's domination and achieve an agreement that is fair (Corcoran and Melamed 1990; Marthaler 1989). In cases where parents are unable to negotiate terms of a settlement regarding custody and access via mediation, the judicial system may be the only means to resolve such disputes.

Therapeutic Implications: Divorced Fathers and Families

The study has identified non-custodial divorced fathers, particularly those who have become disengaged from their children's lives, as a large and vulnerable population that warrants closer therapeutic attention from the helping professions. Despite the recognition that fathers are an integral part of the families with whom therapeutic agents work in a variety of practice settings, fathers in general are largely underrepresented as clientele in these settings. This is particularly pronounced in the case of non-custodial divorced fathers, who are very often excluded from therapy.

Existing clinical and research literature on men as fathers has described the absence of a "fit" between fathers and therapeutic agents as emanating from two sources: the characteristics of men and fathers themselves (their resistance to counselling and therapy) and aspects of the therapeutic process that have failed to successfully engage fathers (Forster 1988; Ambrose et al. 1983).

It has been suggested that patterns of traditional gender-role socialization, directing men towards self-sufficiency and control, independent problem solving, and emotional restraint, have worked against fathers' abilities to acknowledge personal difficulties and request help. The present study found that a fear of self-disclosure and a feeling of disloyalty to one's family in exposing family problems were common. A fear of losing control over one's life and the need to present an image of control or a "facade of coping" in the form of exterior calm, strength, and rationality despite considerable inner turmoil were described by a large number of fathers in the sample. Recent investigations of fathers' involvement in clinical settings have revealed that therapeutic agencies do not always consider such psychological obstacles to therapy and are rarely geared to meeting fathers' unique clinical needs. Fathers are often excluded from therapy partly because of a perceived lack of cooperation and partly because their apparent lack of interest is not questioned. Therapists often accept a mother's assertion that a father is "not interested" in the child or in attending therapeutic sessions (Jordan 1985). Therapists themselves are not immune from social expectations of how "reasonable" and "responsible" fathers ought to behave. The behaviour of fathers during divorce in particular can be completely at odds with these expectations, with actions and sentiments ranging from extreme male chauvinism to pathetically helpless and "unmanly" (Forster 1988). Many therapists simply do not acknowledge the extent of divorced fathers' difficulties, pointing to fathers' apparent freedom from responsibility after divorce, in contrast to the more visible difficulties experienced by their former wives and children (Foote 1981).

The first step in meeting the mental health needs of divorced fathers is to recognize that they are significantly affected by divorce and by the threatened or actual loss of their children, which may occasion a grief reaction that contains all of the major elements of bereavement. For many non-custodial fathers, chronic grief ensues, and problematic issues remain unresolved despite the passage of time. Second, it should be acknowledged that fathers have a strong desire and need for regular and frequent contact with their children after divorce. For the great majority of non-custodial fathers, traditional access arrangements are woefully inadequate. Fathers want and are prepared to assume physical care of their children after divorce. A shared custody arrangement is perceived as the optimal post-divorce living arrangement by a significant number of divorced fathers, particularly those who had a comparatively active role to play in their children's lives before divorce. Third, it should be recognized that powerful psychological and structural factors constrain fathers' post-divorce contact with their children, and the combination of these strongly militate against an ongoing father-child relationship. Such recognition requires a reassessment of prevailing assumptions and stereotypes on the part of clinicians, a reconsideration of traditional methods of intervention, and an active program of outreach to engage non-custodial fathers in the therapeutic process.

The therapeutic process can be tailored to meet divorced fathers' individual therapeutic needs in a number of ways. In the present study, fathers identified the need, in the initial and later stages of divorce, for a combination of practical advice (about the options open to them and related legal procedures and practices) and emotional support. Fathers expressed a preference for a directive type of counselling with structured goal-setting and a pragmatic, problem-solving approach rather than one of emotional ventilation or in-depth exploration of dysfunctional family interactions; a stance, according to Blackie and Clark (1987), that reflects their orientation to public arenas characterized by the achievement of measurable goals. They were also, however, seeking an opportunity to talk about their feelings within a sympathetic, nonjudgemental atmosphere with someone able to convey a genuine understanding of their experience of divorce. They spoke of others' lack of understanding and of a general public hostility to their feelings of loss, depression, and victimization. Discussion of such feelings should be encouraged for fathers in therapy, particularly feelings that lie behind their overt anger. Though fathers may present themselves in the therapeutic setting as primarily seeking practical advice and direction, it is important for the therapist to encourage examination of the emotional impact of divorce on the father. The therapist should take the initiative to combat fathers' emotional inexpressiveness (Bowl 1985) by demonstrating a genuine understanding of their feelings, by normalizing the experience of such intense emotions, by stressing the importance of emotional expressiveness and reflective behaviour to those who tend to see problems and solutions in more concrete terms, and by bolstering fathers' self-esteem and their sense of parental identity. Therapists should attempt to look beyond fathers' initial defensive poses, their indirect or often uncooperative manner, or their "everything is fine" demeanor.

As part of the exploration of the emotional aspects of the divorce, the therapist's agenda should include a focus on the children of the marriage. The loss of their children and the pre-divorce father-child relationship is the most salient loss for most non-custodial fathers. Contrary to earlier formulations, a father's grief appears to be primarily linked to the absence of his children. "Child absence syndrome" has been identified within the psychiatric literature:

> To systematize this important constellation of forces is to do no more (and no less) than what has been done for other unique stressors (for example, Holocaust Survivor Syndrome) because they are thought to require special education and sensitivity for their diagnosis, understanding, and more sophisticated management (Jacobs 1986a:46)

After divorce, non-custodial fathers locate themselves at different points along the bereavement continuum: some fathers are able to arrive at a resolution of their grief, but others remain "stuck" at an earlier stage of the grieving process. It should be noted, however, that chronic grief, which involves intense and prolonged mourning and depression, is characteristic of disengaged fathers previously highly involved with and attached to their children. Clinicians need to be aware that such depression is not always overtly manifested. A "façade of coping" or overt anger may mask a prevalent sense of loss and emotional distress. Neither should therapists assume that fathers' grief becomes naturally resolved through the passage of time. Non-custodial fathers are overrepresented in studies of suicide, and clinicians need to be alert to the threat of such a measure. Fantasies of self-destruction are relatively common and should be distinguished from a real plan or an intense impulse to carry out such fantasies (Jacobs 1986a).

Divorce occasions a grief reaction for non-custodial fathers, linked to the loss of their children. Bereavement counselling that gives fathers the "permission" to grieve and frees them to grieve by reassuring them that expressing feelings and "grieving" is a "normal" reaction appears to be an indicated form of therapy. It may be contended, however, that bereavement counselling in the traditional sense is not appropriate for non-custodial fathers, as the objects of their grief are still alive. Giving "permission to grieve" is ethically supportable only if termination of the grieving process is foreseeable. The resolution of grief for disengaged fathers, however, is highly problematic and probably highly resistant to psychotherapy. Thus a number of fathers in the study commented on the unhelpful nature of traditional counselling services when they had been sought; few felt that their grief could be resolved without reference to ways of resurrecting their relationship with their children.

The most pressing need of non-custodial fathers, particularly those who were highly involved with and attached to their children before divorce, is for a continued and meaningful involvement with their children. *In most cases,* clinicians have a professional responsibility to support the active involvement of non-custodial fathers in their children's lives, and the primary treatment should be the supportive maintenance of the father-child relationship. The clinical picture for fathers is most favourable if child absence does not become a reality— if fathers who had an active role to play in their children's lives can continue a satisfying and unthreatened parental relationship with their children. The picture significantly worsens if child absence becomes routinized. If contact between a father and child has been broken for a prolonged period of time, re-establishing a relationship is likely to be highly problematic for both and may be contraindicated. Early intervention thus becomes critical, as access patterns become established and consolidated in the first six months after separation, and changes to these patterns become more difficult over time, particularly if paternal contact has has been curtailed.

Generally speaking, the role of the therapist towards the non-custodial father should include an educative and advocacy component, with "non-custodial" status in itself being challenged as an appropriate post-divorce role for fathers. Fathers need to be fully informed about alternative post-divorce custodial arrangements and about alternatives to litigation in determining custody and access. They need to be empowered to pursue a continued relationship with their children and to enhance their parenting and co-parenting skills during and after divorce.

Conjoint and Family Therapy

Ideally, the unit of treatment before, during, and after divorce is the family system. In marital and divorce counselling, conjoint counselling is the treatment of choice, because individual therapy may place the therapist in the role of being a judge, or even a catalyst of the divorce. The danger of forming a therapeutic alliance with one partner before the other comes into sessions exists in individual counselling and may increase the polarization of the marital dyad and the possibility of an adversarial dissolution.

The case for conjoint marital and divorce counselling is strong. The cause of marital disruption is more likely to emerge as family transactions are directly observed, and rationalizations and distortions are less likely; communication between the spouses, which will be needed in the post-divorce situation around parenting arrangements, becomes a focus of therapy; countertransference and triangulation of the therapist in the marital conflict is less likely (whereas the impulse to polarize is strong in individual counselling); and the possibility of reconciliation is increased.

In post-divorce counselling and family therapy, because emotional connections continue to exist between both parents and their children, the therapist needs to assist the family to redefine itself as including all family members, with children continuing to have two parents. However, conflicts that arise out of the "unfinished business" between the former spouses can threaten the establishment and maintenance of a post-divorce co-parenting relationship. These dynamics are not visible or may be distorted unless all family members are seen together, and the inclusion of both parents in family therapy or post-divorce counselling can lead to improved relationships between the parents and ultimately improved parenting. In contrast to the position of some family therapists, who treat the mother and children as a unit on the assumption that conjoint therapy would only reinforce antagonism between the former spouses, it is argued here that conjoint counselling after divorce is crucial to therapeutic effectiveness. As in mediation, conjoint counselling should begin by exploring the history of power relations between the couple, bearing in mind the historical inequality in family systems.

Conjoint counselling during and after divorce should primarily focus on assisting both parents to maintain meaningful relationships with their children, and on fostering parental cooperation in this regard. Assisting parents to separate their ongoing parenting responsibilities from residual marital issues and to develop effective conflict-reducing mechanisms may necessitate any of a number of strategies: limiting the frequency of face-to-face encounters between the former spouses; teaching negotiation and planning skills; scheduling and coordination between the two households; encouraging the development of outside relationships; or focusing on the acceptance of the divorce and the related loss of one's marital identity.

The language of the therapist is crucial to the effectiveness of conjoint counselling. Concepts such as "custody" and "access" and the "custodial" and the "non-custodial" parent can lead to an adversarial stance and impede the search for alternate solutions. Language should reflect a shift from "custody" or "ownership" of children to one of "shared parenting" after divorce. A fundamental shift in therapists' statements to families is required, away from concepts such as "Your child needs one parent and one home base," "He needs a familiar place and not be bounced around like a yo-yo," and "A child should live with the mother and have frequent visiting with the father" and towards concepts such as "Children need the two of you to work out their living schedules so that they're consistent and not confusing," "Your child will feel more secure if he sees both of you a great deal and spends some overnights in both homes," and "She can spend more overnights with one of you, although she needs to be with the other a good deal of the time" (Foote, 1981). In his or her use of language, the therapist can actively reinforce a new conceptual way for divorced parents to think and act.

Family Violence

The therapist's agenda should also include a focus on the dynamics of the couple relationship and the nature of parent-child relationships during the marriage. The continued active involvement of both parents in their children's lives, and the need for post-divorce conjoint and family therapy towards this goal, are based on the assumptions that both parents are capable and nurturing caretakers of their children and that neither partner continues to be intimidated by the other after divorce. However, given a patriarchy that condones the use of power to subordinate women, the widespread occurence of violence against women, and the fact that children who witness interparental violence should themselves be considered victims of abuse (Pagelow 1990), divorce mediation and therapeutic programs must explicitly address the issue of family violence and its role in the breakdown of the marriage. The facts that each year four in every thousand Canadian women, aged 16 and over, are subjected to physical and/or sexual assault by spouses, that only 44 percent of these events were reported to police (Statistics Canada 1988), and that male violence escalates upon separation and divorce, with three-fourths of assaults reported to police occurring after separation (Hart 1990), underline the importance of effective screening mechanisms and procedures to ensure the safety of women and children. These include not only therapeutic efforts but protective restraining orders and the option of legal sanctions. In screening, explicit questions need to be posed regarding decision-making, conflict management, and anger expression, as well as specific abusive behaviours (Girdner 1990).

Fathers' denial of responsibility for violent behaviour and resistance to participation in programs for assaultive males, and traditional male roles and needs for control, should be challenged. Family violence is not only a therapeutic problem but is also a legal and political one, and divorce mediation and therapeutic programs should never undermine the use of family violence statutes. Divorce mediation and therapeutic services can thus contribute to the process of changing underlying power imbalances (which may otherwise remain hidden) and can empower victims of domestic violence.

Timing of Therapy

Divorce is both a crisis and a several-staged process for families. The crisis period during divorce (from the point of divorce to approximately six months after) is the optimal time for therapeutic intervention. Counselling early in the divorcing process is crucial to success.

The crisis period during divorce is profoundly stressful for all family members. According to crisis theory, individuals are more susceptible to external influences during a period of disruption than one of relative equilibrium. Therapeutic intervention during crisis helps family members to regain equilibrium by changing their own mode of coping or changing other factors in the situation. The period of disruption may thus be followed by a new, potentially improved adaptation that is qualitatively different from the one preceding it.

Mediation and divorce counselling are most effective during the crisis period of divorce. There exists a fluidity in family relationships in the initial period of divorce (Wallerstein and Kelly 1980), including the father-child relationship; post-divorce relationship patterns become established and consolidated during divorce, and diminished or disrupted fathering later becomes extremely difficult to modify. Therapeutic intervention is thus most effective while the father-child relationship is at its most malleable: the period immediately after divorce, as new relationship patterns are emerging.

Therapeutic intervention should be readily available to families as the marital relationship declines and in the initial stages of divorce. Research has demonstrated that early intervention can be extremely effective in several areas: assisting parents in informing and supporting their children, based on an understanding of the varied responses of children at different ages and stages of development; preparing for economic, social, and psychological changes; separating parenting responsibilities from marital issues; and setting up appropriate plans for the continued care of the children (Saposnek 1983; Irving 1980). Gratifying relationships between parents and children that are established and endured through the first six months of divorce hold the potential for remaining remarkably constant (Wallerstein and Kelly 1980); counselling instituted after the first six months risks dealing with symptomatic behaviours, child alignments, and parenting patterns that have become consolidated and are strongly defended. A delay in counselling also unnecessarily extends confusion and turmoil for family members.

Implications for Clinical Practice and Training

According to Marsh (1987), the relative neglect of fathers by the helping professions is rooted historically in traditional practice models that characterize fathers as peripheral to parenting. Despite a more recent rethinking of traditional theories of child development and psychopathology—with new models of family therapy pointing to the involvement of all family members in therapy—stereotypical assumptions remain widespread towards the non-custodial divorced father. Therapeutic practice with divorcing populations remains largely maternally based, and therapists often accept mothers' accounts of fathers' peripheral roles during the marriage or lack of interest in their children after divorce. Fathers are extremely sensitive to such alignments, and as a result largely consider therapeutic intervention as unhelpful (Ambrose et al., 1983).

The present study has important implications for clinical education. The prevalence of stereotypical assumptions and the lack of knowledge about the needs and experiences of non-custodial fathers call for the development of more specialized knowledge about men, fathers, and the impact of divorce on non-custodial fathers. Because the family system has come to be recognized as a primary unit for intervention, training and practice are required within the helping professions to meet the difficulties in engaging men, fathers, and non-custodial fathers in therapy. Such specialized knowledge, it is argued, must be developed not only through specialized courses in "Men's Studies" but must be integrated into core curricula in the helping professions.

Family Policy Implications

To allow fathers to fully participate in family life, including the care and rearing of children before and after divorce, to facilitate a true sharing of parenting tasks and responsibilities, and to equalize life opportunities outside the family for men and women, institutional change at the governmental, judicial, employment, welfare, and educational levels is essential.

Structures of Employment

Current employment structures and practices strongly mediate against paternal participation in parenting and attempts to equalize family work tasks. To allow shared parenting during marriage and after divorce, restructuring the nature of employment and the material conditions of men's and women's lives is needed. Specifically, two types of structural changes in the workplace are critical: the elimination of gender-based income differentials and occupational segregation, and changes in the nature of the work role itself (Brannen and Moss 1987).

The structure of inequality in employment is such that wage discrimination almost invariably makes men's wages higher than women's, and occupational segregation significantly limits women's employment and career options. Both are powerful structural barriers to fathers' active involvement with their children before and after divorce; ending employment discrimination by ensuring jobs for women with adequate pay and status, with supportive legislation such as equal pay for work of comparable value, is an important measure in promoting paternal participation.

Current employment practices and policies regarding the work role similarly affect the options of women and men in caring for their children and providing economically for their families. Changes on this level are needed to recognize and support the parental role of both mothers and fathers and to facilitate their attempts to combine employment and parenthood. The actual amount of time spent working and the scheduling of work are consistently identified by fathers as inhibiting their participation in parenting tasks. As discussed in Chapter 2, the timing of career demands is such that the greatest work effort is generally required at the earlier stages of a father's work or career. Split work shifts, job sharing schemes, and flexible work schedules continue to be difficult to negotiate. Requirements for geographical mobility pose major problems, particularly for divorced fathers—relocation or frequent travel generally makes shared parenting an unrealistic option.

Several measures can help fathers and mothers to cope with the difficulties of balancing work and family commitments: the availability of decent part-time work without a loss of benefits, job sharing schemes, split work shifts, flexible work hours, shortened working weeks and work days, and the timing of career demands over the life cycle. The provision of parental leave and leave for family reasons have been shown to be particularly effective. Parental leave gives both mothers and fathers the option of caring for their young children; both are entitled to stay at home for a period of time to take sole or principal charge of their children, with pay. Paternal use of the program may be more likely if the payment fathers receive during the leave is not substantially below their usual earnings, if the attitudes of employers and significant others are positive, and if the option of parental leave on a part-time basis is available. Leave for family reasons entitles parents to take time off for a specified number of days each year per child, for reasons such as to attend to children when ill, to attend medical appointments with children, or to visit services such as child-care centres or schools.

Rather than family life being shaped by the needs of employment structures, employment should be shaped to meet the requirements of family life. This can only be effected by public regulation of private employment institutions. Employment policies which assume that parents have an equal responsibility for their children and facilitate the combination of employment and parenthood should be encouraged. The differences in the structural position of men and women in employment, however, need to be confronted first and foremost by legislation. Structures of employment and economic opportunity that favour men are social realities that should be dealt with by government intervention in the first instance.

Child Care Policy

Publicly funded, universally accessible, and quality-ensured child care is also essential for the equalization of employment opportunities for women and men and a more egalitarian division of parenting tasks and responsibilities during marriage and after divorce. Though comprehensive child care programs should be considered as primarily within the jurisdiction of government administrative policy, private employment structures may also be seen as having a responsibility to provide suitable workplace daycare, which could be funded on a cost sharing basis. Another alternative may be the provision of pre-primary school programs for children between 2 and 5 years of age, and more afterschool programs, a relatively cost efficient means of providing high quality care. The creation or expansion of such programs would eliminate the artificial historical dichotomy between traditional child care programs and pre-primary care.

Education: Family Life Curricula

Family life curricula are taught at different stages through the education system. Such programs should be given higher priority than at present, be taught on a continuing basis from the point of entry through the primary and secondary levels, and include ongoing instruction in parenting and child-care skills, interpersonal relationships and communication skills, and the various types of family structures within which children find themselves.

The education system, in training pupils for employment and parenthood, has an important role in promoting gender equality and ending traditional norms that prescribe gender-segregated roles in family and employment structures. Educators must re-examine the ways that children are socialized in the school system. The elimination of gender-stereotyping in textbooks and school curricula is critical. Early exposure should be provided to "nurturing" male models of adulthood (who are sensitive, caring, and able to express their emotions), and male and female pupils should have the opportunity to develop affective and parenting capacities as they get older. Preparation for parenthood should be an essential component of family life education at all levels, focusing on infant and child care, child development, behaviour management, and domestic tasks; actual experience with infants and young children may become part of such a program for older pupils. Preparation for marriage should include the development of communication and relationship skills, and training in problem-solving and conflict resolution while focusing on problems inherent in married life.

The classroom remains a virtually untapped resource for providing divorce-oriented education to children and adolescents, and the topic of divorce has been largely ignored in family life courses. Empathic skills can be taught to teachers and, with appropriate training, family life instructors could be able to offer a constructive program of divorce education.

Teachers and educators need to avoid projecting a negative attitude towards children from divorced families, making certain they are not unduly singled out as "troubled" children. School administrators should be alert to policies regarding children and parents from divorced families developed from a "deviance" perspective or from the assumption that the custodial parent is the only "legitimate" parent after divorce. Given the number of school children from divorced families, forthright, openly stated policies that encourage the involvement of both parents in their children's education are necessary. Schools should not be placed in the position of having to mediate divorced parents' disagreements over access to children's educational records, teacher conferences, or the children themselves. An "open disclosure" policy of relevant educational information to both parents, regardless of custodial status, is recommended.

Parenting Programs

The transition to parenthood is sudden, irrevocable, and generally preceded by little or no training, particularly for males. The education system is the best means to provide such training, but until more comprehensive family life programs are instituted, educational efforts directed towards the adult male population, with and without children, are urgently needed.

Psychoeducational programming for "emergent" fatherhood may be geared towards consciousness raising, attitude change, and goal clarification, or towards the teaching of specific parenting skills. "Consciousness raising" educational efforts may be focused on various areas such as presenting "emergent" and nurturant images and models of fathers in parenting manuals and the media, challenging fathers' and employers' attitudes and beliefs about fathers' commitments to their work roles as their primary obligation to the family, and facilitating social acceptance of shared parenting family structures and of fathers who remain at home with their children. Similarly, a range of child care and child development instructional programs are needed, both in hospitals and as community education initiatives, with target populations that include expectant fathers; fathers of preschool, school-age, and adult children; and divorced fathers.

Particular attention should be directed towards the time of men's transition to parenthood and towards teaching fathers about their newborns, children's normal growth and development, how to promote that development, and how to fully and meaningfully exercise their new role as "fathers." Hospitals have a critical function in this regard: the provision of facilities for expectant fathers and guidance and education for them; involvement of fathers in childbirth; the provision of live-in facilities for new fathers; post-partum instruction about child care; and involvement of fathers in all aspects of routine daily care for their newborns in hospital all facilitate active paternal involvement in the future. Failure to make such provisions contributes to a father's feelings of peripherality at the earliest stages and may well have negative repercussions on the later development of the father-child relationship.

Conclusion

Reconceptualizing "Divorce"

It is now generally recognized that the difficulties experienced by family members upon divorce are not the result of divorce per se but are associated with the disruption of interpersonal relationships, particularly the discontinuity in parent-child attachments, that attend divorce. Divorce in itself is thus now viewed less as an indicator of pathology, but as a normal developmental occurrence in people's lives which, despite the emphasis on negative outcomes in the literature, has considerable potential as a means for achieving growth (Ahrons 1981).

A positive framework for clinical intervention with divorcing and divorced families should not theoretically regard divorce from a "deviance" perspective but should seek to "normalize" the event of divorce for family members. An essential element of "normalizing" divorce is the provision of a wide range of options in post-divorce family arrangements that will ensure the maintenance of children's active relationships with both parents. Divorce is a crisis in the normal life cycle of a family that requires a rearrangement of relationships. The maintenance of continued meaningful parent-child relationships for both parents within a mutually supportive co-parenting relationship significantly reduces the crisis potential associated with divorce for all family members.

Reconceptualizing "the Divorced Family"

In light of the evidence of the salutary effects of sharing care of children after divorce for mothers, fathers, and children, a strong case may be made for shared parenting as a desired norm for post-divorce families. Ahrons (1980) conceptualizes shared parenting as a "bi-nuclear family system," to be thought of as an organic unit, a family system consisting of two interrelated households, maternal and paternal, that are the nuclei of a child's "family of orientation." Rather than "ending" a family, divorce alters the nature of family roles and relationships by initiating a process of family change. It is a crisis of family transition resulting in structural changes in the family system. The issue for families (and those working with families) should not be *whether* divorced parents should share parenting, but *how* they can effectively do so, within a mutually supportive and cooperative relationship. The main purpose of intervention with a family during divorce thus becomes the redefinition of family roles, relationships, and boundaries to allow the family to continue as a divorced family system. Intervention should focus primarily on the clarification of boundaries so that the spousal role does not "contaminate" the co-parental role, on helping parents to separate their previous marital conflicts from their ongoing parental responsibilities.

"The divorced family" thus may be viewed as a dynamic and evolving institution able to take many forms, with the core of the family being not the marriage, but the parent-child bond. Such a reconceptualization considers families to be not immutable structures, but social systems operating within many configurations. Divorce thus does not lead to dissolution, but to other variants of "the family."

Reconceptualizing "the Divorced Father"

Conceptualizations of men as primarily bound to the sphere of employment and of women as bound to the realm of the family as being the characteristic of all fathers and mothers deny the existence of a heterogeneity of "fathering" and "mothering" roles in families, and they also deny the values, sentiments, attachments, and behaviours revealed by the fathers in this study. The empirical evidence that men are capable of loving and nurturing relationships with their children, that children form powerful attachment bonds with both of their parents, and that strong father-child relationships create richer possibilities for children's development all stand in sharp contrast to current practices and policies based on traditional conceptualizations.

Given the heterogeneity of fatherhood roles and patterns today, there is substantial evidence that fathers' lives generally contain greater attachments and are more profoundly affected by fatherhood than is usually assumed. For those fathers who are highly involved with and attached to their children within the marriage, divorce can have disastrous consequences in the form of the actual or threatened loss of one's children and the pre-divorce father-child relationship. Such fathers, facing divorce, desperately want to maintain a meaningful relationship with their children, but the nature of traditional custody and access arrangements prohibit such a relationship. For these fathers, limited access does not allow sufficient opportunity for the variety and richness of contact that is necessary to sustain complex family relationships. Fathers may see at least partial physical custody of their children after divorce as the only way for them to remain as "real fathers," actively responsible for and committed to the well-being of their children.

The disengagement of previously highly involved and attached fathers is likely to continue as long as "non-custodial" status applies. It is the group of previously highly involved men who stand to lose the most following divorce. For these fathers, "non-custodial fatherhood" is a contradiction in terms. For them, "fatherhood" involves the continuation of the full complement of tasks, responsibilities, and privileges of the parent role, whereas "non-custodial" imposes a restriction, limitation, or cessation of those same functions.

We now have a considerable body of evidence on which to base what is in "the best interests of the child" after divorce. The most important factors in children's post-divorce adjustment have been shown to be, for the great majority of children, measures to provide them with comfort and appropriate understanding, economic stability, a supportive co-parental relationship between the parents, and the protection of continuity in their relationships with both parents. The latter has been shown to be particularly critical—in assessing the relative importance of these factors, Lund's (1987) research isolated paternal involvement as the most salient variable in children's post-divorce adjustment. According to Richards (1989:84), although "children do least well when there is a lot of conflict between parents during and after the divorce . . . this seems to be because inter-parental conflict is very corrosive of parent-child relationships. Where these relationships are maintained despite the conflict, children appear to be insulated from its negative effects." Just as fathers suffer the effects of child absence during and after divorce, so children experience the absence of their fathers. Just as fathers' identities are tied to their parenting role, so children's self-images are firmly linked with their relationships with their fathers. A divorced father's emotional significance to his children does not diminish, despite infrequent or lost contact. The most stressed children have been shown to be the ones whose relationship with their now-absent father was warm and intimate before divorce (Wallerstein and Kelly 1980; Hetherington et al. 1978).

Enabling fathers to continue to develop such relationships within and beyond marriage should remain a top priority. The importance of nurturant father-child relationships is being encouraged as a crucial factor for the development of "masculinity" as something less coercive and oppressive to women, children, and men themselves, and as part of the ideological struggle to create richer possibilities in breaking down the polarity between "masculinity" and "femininity" (Segal 1990). Such relationships before and after divorce, however, are actively constrained within prevailing structures of employment, modes of custody and access determination, and traditional family structures. Men's lives don contain profound emotional attachments to their children. Strong work-family conflicts for men in two-parent families and the profound sense of loss felt by non-custodial fathers disengaged from their children's lives are powerful illustrations of the costs some men pay for the power and privileges bestowed upon them by patriarchal power structures.

Notes

[1] All following references to "divorce" are meant to refer to the final parental separation.

[2] Most of the table following are based on post-coded categories, created by the post-coding of fathers' responses to open-ended questions.

[3] Tables 4 and 5 are listed according to column percentages. Significance level is based upon chi square approximation.

[4] One (disengaged) father did not know the details of the legal access determination and was excluded from the present analysis.

[5] Fourteen contact fathers indicated that their ex-wives had in some way discouraged contact; two stated that they had both encouraged and discouraged.

[6] Fifty-six of the eighty fathers indicated that their former spouses had in some way discouraged father-child contact after divorce.

Select Bibliography

Abarbanel, A. 1979. "Shared Parenting After Separation and Divorce: A Study of Joint Custody." *American Journal of Orthopsychiatry* 49(4).

Ahrons, C.R. 1983. "Predictors of Parental Involvement Postdivorce: Mothers' and Fathers' Perceptions." *Journal of Divorce* 6(3).

——. 1981. "The Continuing Coparental Relationship Between Divorced Spouses." *American Journal of Orthopsychiatry* 51(3).

——. 1980. "Divorce: A Crisis of Family Transition and Change." *Family Relations* 29.

Aldous, J. 1981. "From Dual-Earner to Dual-Career Families and Back Again." *Journal of Family Issues* 2.

Ambert, A. 1980. *Divorce in Canada*. Don Mills: Academic Press.

Ambrose, P., J. Harper, and R. Pemberton. 1983. *Surviving Divorce: Men Beyond Marriage*. Sussex: Harvester Press.

August, E. 1985. *Men's Studies: A Selected and Annotated Interdisciplinary Bibliography*, Littleton, Conn.: Libaries Unlimited.

Backett, K. 1987. "The Negotiation of Fatherhood." In C. Lewis and M. O'Brien (eds.), *Reassessing Fatherhood*. London: Sage.

——. 1982. *Mothers and Fathers: A Study of the Development and Negotiation of Parental Behaviour*. London: Macmillan.

Bala, N. 1987. "Family Law in the United States and Canada: Different Visions of Similar   Realities." *International Journal of Law and the Family* 1(1).

Beail, N., and J. McGuire. 1982. "Fathers, the Family, and Society: The Tide of Change." In N. Beail and J. McGuire (eds.), *Fathers: Psychological Perspectives*. London: Junction Books.

Beail, N., and J. McGuire, eds. 1982. *Fathers: Psychological Perspectives*. London: Junction Books.

Benokraitis, N. 1985. "Fathers in the Dual-Earner Family." In S.M.H. Hanson and F.W. Bozett (eds.), *Dimensions of Fatherhood*. Beverly Hills: Sage.

Benson, L. 1968. *Fatherhood: A Sociological Perspective.* New York: Random House.

Berger, M. 1979. "Men's New Family Roles: Some Implications for Therapists." *Family Coordinator* 28(4).

Berk, S.F. 1985. *The Gender Factory.* New York: Plenum Press.

Berman, W.H., and D.C. Turk. 1983. "Adaptation to Divorce: Problems and Coping Strategies." In H. Olson and B.C. Miller (eds.), *Family Studies Review Yearbook.* Vol. 1. Beverly Hills: Sage.

Blackie, S., and D. Clark. 1987. "Men in Marriage Counselling." In C. Lewis and M. O'Brien (eds.), *Reassessing Fatherhood.* London: Sage.

Blades, J. 1984. "Mediation: An Old Art Revitalized." *Mediation Quarterly* 3.

Bloom, B.L. 1975. *Changing Patterns of Psychiatric Care.* New York: Human Science Press.

Bloom, B.L., S.J. Asher, and S.W. White. 1978. "Marital Disruption as a Stressor: A Review and Analysis." *Psychological Bulletin* 85(4).

Bloom, B.L., and W.F. Hodges. 1981. "The Predicament of the Newly Separated." *Community Mental Health Journal* 17(4).

Bloom, B.L., S.W. White, and S.J. Asher. 1979. "Marital Disruption as a Stressful Life Event." In G. Levinger and O.C. Moles (eds.), *Divorce and Separation.* New York: Basic Books.

Bohannan, P., ed. 1970. *Divorce and After.* Garden City: Doubleday.

Bowl, R. 1985. *Changing the Nature of Masculinity - A Task for Social Work?* Social Work Monographs. Norwich: University of East Anglia.

Bowlby, J. 1977. "The Making and Breaking of Affectional Bonds." *British Journal of Psychiatry* 130.

Bowman, M.E., and C.R. Ahrons. 1985. "Impact of Legal Custody Status on Fathers' Parenting Postdivorce." *Journal of Marriage and the Family* 47(2).

Brannen, J., and P. Moss. 1987. "Fathers in Dual-Earner Households: Through Mothers' Eyes." In C. Lewis and M. O'Brien (eds.), *Reassessing Fatherhood.* London: Sage.

Bresee, P., G.B. Stearns, B.H. Bess, and L.S. Packer. 1986. "Allegations of Child Sexual Abuse in Child Custody Disputes: A Therapeutic Assessment Model." *American Journal of Orthopsychiatry* 56(4).

Brod, H. 1987. "A Case for Men's Studies." In M.S. Kimmel (ed.), *Changing Men.* Beverly Hills: Sage.

Brotsky, M., S. Steinman, and S. Zemmelman. 1988. "Joint Custody Through Mediation Reviewed."*Conciliation Courts Review* 26(2).

Burgess, E.W., H.J. Locke, and M.M. Thomes. 1971.*The Family.* New York: Van Nostrand Reinhold.

Burgoyne, J., and D. Clark. 1984. *Making a Go of It: A Study of Stepfamilies in Sheffield.* London: Routledge and Kegan Paul.

Burgoyne, J., R. Ormrod, and M. Richards. 1987. *Divorce Matters.* Harmondsworth: Penguin.

Calvin, D.A. 1981. "Joint Custody as Family and Social Policy." In I.R. Stuart and L.E. Abt (eds.), *Children of Separation and Divorce.* New York: Van Nostrand Reinhold.

Charnas, J.F. 1983. "Joint Child Custody Counselling: Divorce 1980s Style." *Social Casework* 64(9).

Chesler, P. 1986. *Mothers on Trial.* New York: McGraw-Hill.

Chiriboga, D.A., A. Coho, J.A. Stein, and J. Roberts. 1979. "Divorce, Stress, and Social Supports: A Study in Help-Seeking Behaviour." *Journal of Divorce* 3.

Clingempeel, W.G., and N.D. Reppucci. 1982. "Joint Custody After Divorce: Major Issues and Goals for Research." *Psychological Bulletin* 91(1).

Cohen, T.F. 1987. "Remaking Men." *Journal of Family Issues* 8(1).

Coleman, M.T. 1988. "The Division of Household Labour: Suggestions for Future Empirical Consideration and Theoretical Development." *Journal of Family Issues* 9(1).

Conway, F. 1990. *The Canadian Family in Crisis.* Toronto: Lorimer.

Corcoran, K., and J.C. Melamed. 1990. "From Coercion to Empowerment: Spousal Abuse and Mediation." *Mediation Quarterly* 7 (4).

Crosby, J.F., S.K. Lybarger, and R.L. Mason. 1987. "The Grief Resolution Process in Divorce: Phase II." *Journal of Divorce* 10(1-2).

Crosby, J.F., B. Gage, and M. Raymond. 1983. "The Grief Resolution Process in Divorce." *Journal of Divorce* 7(1).

David, D.S., and R. Brannon, eds. 1976. *The Forty-Nine Percent Majority: The Male Sex Role.* Reading, Mass.: Addison-Wesley.

Davis, G., and K. Bader. 1985. "In-court Mediation: The Consumer View." *Family Law* 15(1).

Davis, G., A. MacLeod, and M. Murch. 1982. "Divorce and the Resolution of Conflict." *Law Society Gazette* 40(1).

Department of Justice Canada. 1990. *Evaluation of the Divorce Act.* Ottawa: Bureau of Review.

Derdeyn, A.P. 1977. "Child Custody Contests in Historical Perspective." In S. Chess and A. Thomas (eds.), *Annual Progress in Child Psychiatry and Child Development.* New York: Brunner/Mazel.

——. 1976. "A Consideration of Legal Issues in Child Custody Contests: Implications for Change." *Archives of General Psychiatry* 33.

Derdeyn, A., and E. Scott. 1984. "Joint Custody: A Critical Analysis and Appraisal." *American Journal of Orthopsychiatry* 54.

Deutsch, M. 1973. *The Resolution of Conflict: Constructive and Destructive Processes.* New Haven, Conn: Yale University Press.

Duryee, M.A. 1985. "Public-Sector Mediation: A Report from the Courts." *Mediation Quarterly* 8.

Eekelaar, J. 1984. *Family Law and Social Policy .* Second edition. London: Weidenfeld and Nicolson.

Eekelaar, J., and E. Clive. 1977. *Custody After Divorce.* Oxford: Centre for Socio-Legal Studies.

Ehrensaft, D. 1980. "When Men and Women Mother." *Socialist Review* 49.

Eichler, M. 1983. *Families in Canada Today.* Toronto: Gage.

Elkin, M. 1987. "Joint Custody: Affirming that Parents and Families are Forever." *Social Work* 32(1).

——. 1978. "Reflections on Joint Custody and Family Law." Editorial. *Conciliation Courts Review* 16(3).

——. 1977. "Postdivorce Counselling in a Conciliation Court." *Journal of Divorce* 1(1).

——. 1973. "Conciliation Courts: The Reintegration of Disintegrating Families." *The Family Coordinator* 22.

Elwork, A., and M.R. Smuckler. 1988. "Developing Training and Practice Standards for Custody Mediators." *Conciliation Courts Review* 26(2).

Engram, P.S. and J.R. Markowitz. 1985. "Ethical Issues in Mediation." *Mediation Quarterly* 8.

Erikson, E.H. 1959. *Identity and the Life Cycle.* New York: International University Press.

Fein, R.A. 1978. "Research on Fathering: Social Policy and an Emergent Perspective." *Journal of Social Issues* 34(1).

Feldberg, R., and E. Glenn. 1979. "Male and Female: Job vs. Gender Models in the Sociology of Work, *Social Problems* 26.

Felner, R.D., L. Terre, J. Primavera, S.S. Farber, and T.A. Bishop. 1985. "Child Custody: Practices and Perspectives of Legal Professionals." *Journal of Clinical Child Psychology* 14(1).

Fineman, M. 1988. "Dominant Discourse, Professional Language, and Legal Change in Child   Custody Decisionmaking." *Harvard Law Review* 101(4).

Foldberg, J., ed. 1984. *Joint Custody and Shared Parenting.* Washington, D.C.: Bureau of National Affairs.

——. 1981. "The Changing Family—Implications for the Law." *Conciliation Courts Review* 19.

Foldberg, J., and M. Graham. 1981. "Joint Custody of Children Following Divorce." In H.H. Irving (ed.), *Family Law.* Toronto: Carswell.

Foldberg, J. and A. Taylor. 1984. *Mediation: A Comprehensive Guide to Resolving Conflicts Without Litigation.* San Francisco: Jossey-Bass.

Foote, C.E. 1988. "Recent State Responses to Separation and Divorce in Canada." *Canadian Social Work Review* 5.

——. 1981. "Life After Divorce for Non-Custodial Parents." Unpublished Master's thesis. Calgary: University of Calgary, Faculty of Social Welfare.

Forster, J. 1988. *Divorce Advice and Counselling for Men.* Edinburgh: Scottish Marriage Guidance Council.

——. 1982. *Divorce Conciliation: A Study of Services in England and Abroad, With Implications for Scotland.* University of Edinburgh: Department of Social Administration.

Foster, H.H., and D.J. Freed. 1980. "Joint Custody: Legislative Reform." *Trial* 16.

Fox, G.L. 1985. "Noncustodial Fathers." In S.M.H. Hanson and F.W. Bozett (eds.), *Dimensions of Fatherhood.* Beverly Hills: Sage.

Franklin, R.L. and B. Hibbs. 1983. "Child Custody in Transition." In D.H. Olson and B.C. Miller (eds.), *Family Studies Review Yearbook.* Vol. 1. Beverly Hills: Sage.

Friedman, H.J. 1980. "The Father's Parenting Experience in Divorce." *American Journal of Orthopsychiatry* 137.

Furstenberg, F., C.W. Nord, J.L. Peterson, and N. Zill. 1983. "The Life Course of Children of Divorce: Marital Disruption and Parental Contact." *American Sociological Review* 48.

Furstenberg, F., and G.B. Spanier. 1984. *Recycling the Family: Marriage After Divorce.* Beverly Hills: Sage.

Garnets, L., and J.H. Pleck. 1979. "Sex Role Identity, Androgyny and Sex-Role Transcendence: A Sex-Role Strain Analysis." *Psychology of Women Quarterly* 3.

Gersick, K.E. 1979. "Fathers by Choice: Divorced Men Who Receive Custody of their Children." In G. Levinger and O.C. Moles (eds.), *Divorce and Separation*. New York: Basic Books.

——. 1975. "Fathers by Choice: Characteristics of Men Who Do and Do Not Seek Custody of their Children Following Divorce." Ph.D. dissertation, Harvard University.

Girdner, L.K. 1990. "Mediation Triage: Screening for Spouse Abuse in Divorce Mediation." *Mediation Quarterly* 7 (4).

Giveans, D.L., and M.K. Robinson. 1985. "Fathers and the Pre-School Child." In S.M.H Hanson and F.W. Bozett (eds.), *Dimensions of Fatherhood*. Beverly Hills: Sage.

Glick, P. 1979. "Children of Divorced Parents in Demographic Perspective." *Journal of Social Issues* 35(4).

Goetting, A. 1981. "Divorce Outcome Research: Issues and Perspectives." *Journal of Family Issues* 2.

Goldstein, J., A. Freud, and A.J. Solnit. 1973. *Beyond the Best Interests of the Child*. New York: The Free Press.

Grebe, S.C. 1976. "Issues of Separation and Loss in Custody Mediation." *Conciliation Courts Review* 24(2).

Greif, J. 1979. "Fathers, Children, and Joint Custody." *American Journal of Orthopsychiatry* 49.

——. 1977. "Child Absence: Fathers' Perceptions of their Relationship to their Children Subsequent to Divorce." D.S.W. dissertation, Adelphi University.

Grubb, W.N., and M. Lazerson. 1984. "Gender Roles and the State." In K.M Borman, D. Quarm, and S. Gideonse (eds.), *Women in the Workplace: Effects on Families*. Norwood, N.J.: Ablex.

Hagen, J.L. 1987. "Proceed with Caution: Advocating Joint Custody." *Social Work* 32(1).

Hanson, S.M.H. 1985. "Single Custodial Fathers." In S.M.H. Hanson and F.W. Bozett (eds.), *Dimensions of Fatherhood*. Beverly Hills: Sage.

Hanson, S.M.H., and F.W. Bozett, eds. 1985. *Dimensions of Fatherhood*. Beverly Hills: Sage.

Hart, B.J. 1990. "Gentle Jeopardy: The Further Endangerment of Battered Women and Children in Custody Mediation." *Mediation Quarterly* 7 (4).

Haskey, J. 1982. "The Proportion of Marriages Ending in Divorce." *Population Trends* 27.

Hearn, J. 1987. *The Gender of Oppression: Men, Masculinity and the Critique of Marxism*. Brighton: Wheatsheaf Books.

Hess, R.D., and K.A. Camara. 1979. "Post-Divorce Family Relationships as Mediating Factors in the Consequences of Divorce for Children." *Journal of Social Issues* 35(4).

Hetherington, E.M., M. Cox, and R. Cox. 1978. "The Aftermath of Divorce." In J.H. Stevens Jr. and M. Mathews (eds.), *Mother-Child, Father-Child*

Relations. Washington: National Association for the Education of Young Children.

——. 1976. "Divorced Fathers." *Family Coordinator* 26(6).

Hirst, S.R., and G.W. Smiley. 1984. "The Access Dilemma: A Study of Access Patterns Following Marriage Breakdown." *Conciliation Courts Review* 22(1).

Hochschild, A., and A. Machung. 1989. *The Second Shift: Inside the Two-Job Marriage.* New York: Penguin.

Hoffman, L.W. 1977. "Changes in Family Roles, Socialization, and Sex Differences." *American Psychologist* 32.

Huntington, D.S. 1986. "Fathers: The Forgotten Figures in Divorce." In J.W. Jacobs (ed.), *Divorce and Fatherhood.* Los Angeles: American Psychiatric Press.

Irving, H.H. 1980. *Divorce Mediation: The Rational Alternative.* Toronto: Personal Library.

Irving, H.H., ed. 1981. *Family Law: An Interdisciplinary Perspective.* Toronto: Carswell.

Irving, H.H., and M. Benjamin. 1987. *Family Mediation: Theory and Practice of Dispute Resolution.* Toronto: Carswell.

Irving, H.H., M. Benjamin, P.E. Bohm, and G. MacDonald. 1981. "A Study of Conciliation Counselling in the Family Court of Toronto." In H.H. Irving (ed.), *Family Law.* Toronto: Carswell.

Irving, H.H., M. Benjamin, and N. Trocme. 1984. "Shared Parenting: An Empirical Analysis Utilizing a Large Data Base." *Family Process* 23(4).

Irving, H.H., and P.E. Bohm. 1981. "An Interdisciplinary Approach to Family Dispute Resolution." In H.H. Irving (ed.), *Family Law.* Toronto: Carswell.

Isaacs, M.B. 1981. "Treatment for Families of Divorce: A Systems Model of Prevention." In I.R. Stuart and L.E. Abt (eds.), *Children of Separation and Divorce.* New York: Van Nostrand Reinhold.

Jacobs, J.W. 1986. "Involuntary Child Absence Syndrome: An Affliction of Divorcing Fathers." In J.W. Jacobs (ed.), *Divorce and Fatherhood.* Los Angeles: American Psychiatric Press.

Jacobs, J.W., ed. 1986. *Divorce and Fatherhood.* Los Angeles: American Psychiatric Press.

James, A., and K. Wilson. 1984. "The Trouble with Access." *British Journal of Social Work* 14(5).

Johnston, J.R., and L.E.G. Campbell. 1988. *Impasses of Divorce: The Dynamics and Resolution of Family Conflict .* New York: The Free Press.

Jordan, P. 1985. *The Effects of Marital Separation on Men.* Sydney: Family Court of Australia.

Jump, T.L., and L. Haas. 1987. "Fathers in Transition: Dual-Career Fathers Participating in Child Care." In M.S. Kimmel (ed.), *Changing Men.* Beverly Hills: Sage.

Kamo, Y. 1988. "Determinants of Household Division of Labor: Resources, Power, and Ideology." *Journal of Family Issues* 9(2).

Kelly, J. 1983. "Mediation and Psychotherapy: Distinguishing the Differences." *Mediation Quarterly* 1.

Kelly, J. 1981. "The Visiting Relationship After Divorce: Research Findings and Clinical Observations" In I.R. Stuart and L.E. Abt (eds.), *Children of Separation and Divorce*. New York: Van Nostrand Reinhold.

Keshet, J.F. and K.M. Rosenthal. 1978. "Fathering After Marital Separation." *Social Work* 23(1).

Kimmel, M.S. 1987. "Rethinking 'Masculinity': New Directions in Research." In M.S. Kimmel (ed.), *Changing Men*. Beverly Hills: Sage.

Kimmel, M.S., ed. 1987. *Changing Men*. Beverly Hills: Sage.

Koopman, E.J., E.J. Hunt, and V. Stafford. 1984. "Child Related Agreements in Mediated and Non-Mediated Divorce Settlements: A Preliminary Examination and Discussion of Implications." *Conciliation Courts Review* 22(1).

——. 1987. "Clinical Implications of Existing Research on Divorce Mediation." *American Journal of Family Therapy* 15(1).

Kressel, K. 1980. "Patterns of Coping in Divorce and Some Implications for Clinical Practice." *Family Relations* 29(2).

——. In press. "The 'Disengaged' Noncustodial Father: Implications for Social Work Practice with the Divorced Family." *Social Work*.

Kruk, E. 1993. "Promoting Cooperative Parenting After Separation: A Therapeutic/ Interventionist Model of Family Mediation." *Journal of Family Therapy* 15(3).

Kruk, E. 1992a. "Child Custody Determination: An Analysis of the Legal Model, Legal Practices, and Experiences of Male Participants in the Process." *Journal of Men's Studies* 1(2).

——. 1992b. "Psychological and Structural Factors Contributing to the Disengagement of Noncustodial Fathers After Divorce." *Family and Conciliation Courts Review* 29(2).

——. 1991a. "Discontinuity Between Pre- and Post-divorce Father-child Relationships: New Evidence Regarding Paternal Disengagement." *Journal of Divorce and Remarriage* 16.

——. 1991b. "The Greif Reaction of Noncustodial Fathers Subsequent to Divorce." *Men's Studies Review* 8(2).

Kubler-Ross, E. 1953. *On Death and Dying*. New York: Doubleday.

Lamb, M.E., ed. 1987. *The Father's Role: Cross-cultural Perspectives*. Hillsdale, N.J.: Erlbaum.

——. 1986. *The Father's Role: Applied Perspectives*. New York: Wiley.

——. 1981. "Fathers and Child Development: An Integrative Overview." In M.E. Lamb (ed.), *The Role of the Father in Child Development* . Second edition. New York: Wiley.

——. 1975. "Fathers: Forgotten Contributors to Child Development." *Human Development* 18.

Lamb, M.E., T.H. Pleck, and J.A. Levine. 1987. "Effects of Increased Paternal Involvement on Fathers and Mothers." In C. Lewis and M. O'Brien (eds.), *Reassessing Fatherhood*. London: Sage.

Lamb, M.E., and A. Sagi, eds. 1983. *Fatherhood and Family Policy*. Hillsdale, N.J.: Erlbaum.

LaRossa, R. 1988. "Fatherhood and Social Change." *Family Relations* 37.

Lein, L. 1979. "Male Participation in Home Life: Impact of Social Supports and Breadwinner Responsibility on the Allocation of Tasks." *Family Coordinator* 28(4).

Levinger, G., and O.C. Moles, eds. 1979. *Divorce and Separation*. New York: Basic Books.

Levy, A.M. 1986. "Psychopathological Responses to Threatened Custody Loss." *Journal of Psychiatry and Law* 14(3-4).

Lewis, C. 1986. *Becoming a Father*. Milton Keynes: Open University Press.

Lewis, C., and M. O'Brien. 1987. "Constraints on Fathers: Research, Theory and Clinical Practice." In C. Lewis and M. O'Brien (eds.), *Reassessing Fatherhood*. London: Sage.

Lewis, C., and M. O'Brien, eds. 1987. *Reassessing Fatherhood*. London: Sage.

Lewis, R.A. 1986a. "Men's Changing Roles in the Marriage and the Family." *Marriage and Family Review* 9(3-4).

——. 1986b. "What Men Get Out of Marriage and Parenthood." In R.A. Lewis and R.E. Salt (eds.), *Men in Families*. Beverly Hills: Sage.

Lewis, R.A., and J.H. Pleck. 1979. "Men's Role in the Family." *Family Coordinator* 28(4).

Lewis, R.A., and R.E. Salt, eds. 1986. *Men in Families*. Beverly Hills: Sage.

Losh-Hesselbart, S. 1987. "Development of Gender Roles." In M.B. Sussman and S.K. Steinmetz (eds.), *Handbook of Marriage and the Family*. New York: Plenum Press.

Lowe, N.Y. 1982. "The Legal Status of Fathers: Past and Present." In L. McKee and M. O'Brien (eds.), *The Father Figure*. London: Tavistock.

Luepnitz, D.A. 1982. *Child Custody*. Lexington, Mass.: Lexington Books.

Lund, M. 1987. "The Non-Custodial Father: Common Challenges in Parenting After Divorce." In C. Lewis and M. O'Brien (eds.), *Reassessing Fatherhood*. London: Sage.

Maidment, S. 1984. *Child Custody and Divorce*. London: Croom Helm.

Marsh, P. 1987. "Social Work and Fathers: An Exclusive Practice?" In C. Lewis and M. O'Brien (eds.), *Reassessing Fatherhood*. London: Sage.

Marthaler, D. 1989. "Successful Mediation with Abusive Couples." *Mediation Quarterly* 23.

Martin, J., and C. Roberts. 1984. *Women and Employment: A Lifetime Perspective*. London: HMSO.

McIsaac, H. 1985. "Confidentiality: An Exploration of Issues." *Mediation Quarterly* 8.

McKee, L. and M. O'Brien. 1982. "The Father Figure: Some Current Orientations and Historical Perspectives." In L. McKee and M. O'Brien (eds.), *The Father Figure*. London: Tavistock.

McKee, L., and M. O'Brien, eds. 1982. *The Father Figure*. London: Tavistock.

McWhinney, R. 1988. "Issues in the Provision and Practice of Family Mediation." *Conciliation Courts Review* 26(2).

Merton, R.K. 1968. *Social Theory and Social Structure*. Glencoe, Ill.: Free Press.

Mitchell, A. 1985. *Children in the Middle*. London: Tavistock.

Mnookin, R.H., and L. Kornhauser. 1979. "Bargaining in the Shadow of the Law: The Case of Divorce." *Yale Law Journal* 88.

Moreland, J., and A.I. Schwebel. 1981. "A Gender Role Transcendent Perspective on Fathering." *The Counseling Psychologist* 9(4).

Mortimer, J.T., and G. Sorensen. 1984. "Men, Women, Work, and Family." In K.M. Borman, D. Quarm, and S. Gideonse (eds.), *Women in the Workplace: Effects on Families*. Norwood, N.J.: Ablex.

Moss, P., and J. Brannen. 1987. "Fathers and Employment." In C. Lewis and M. O'Brien (eds.), *Reassessing Fatherhood*. London: Sage.

Murch, M. 1980. *Justice and Welfare in Divorce*. London: Sweet and Maxwell.

Myers, M.F. 1989. *Men and Divorce*. New York: Guilford Press.

Nehls, N., and M. Morgenbesser. 1980. "Joint Custody: An Exploration of the Issues." *Family Process* 19.

Noble, D. 1983. "Custody Contest: How to Divide and Reassemble a Child." *Social Casework* 64(7).

O'Brien, M. 1982. "The Working Father." In N. Beail and J. McGuire (eds.), *Fathers: Psychological Perspectives*. London: Junction Books.

Ogus, A., J. Walker, and M. Jones-Lee. 1989. *The Costs and Effectiveness of Family Conciliation*. London: The Lord Chancellor's Department, Law Commission.

Pagelow, M. 1990. "Effects of Domestic Violence on Children and Their Consequences for Custody and Visitation Agreements." *Mediation Quarterly* 7 (4).

Parke, R.D. 1981. *Fathering*. London: Fontana.

Parke, R.D., and D.B. Sawin. 1976. "The Father's Role in Infancy: A Re-Evaluation." *Family Coordinator* 25(6).

Parkes, C.M. 1986. *Bereavement: Studies of Grief in Adult Life*. Second edition. Harmondsworth: Pelican.

Parkes, C.M., and R.S. Weiss, 1983. *Recovery from Bereavement*. New York: Basic Books.

Parkinson, L. 1987. "Fathers and Conciliation Services." In C. Lewis and M. O'Brien (eds.), *Reassessing Fatherhood*. London: Sage.

——. 1986. *Conciliation in Separation and Divorce*. Beckenham: Croom Helm.

Parsons, T., and R.F. Bales. 1955. *Family, Socialization and the Interaction Process* . New York: Free Press.

Pearson, J., and N. Thoennes, eds. 1984. *Final Report of the Divorce Mediation Research Project*. Denver: Association of Family and Conciliation Courts Research Unit.

Pedersen, F.A. 1985. "Research and the Father: Where Do We Go From Here?" In S.M.H. Hanson and F.W. Bozett (eds.), *Dimensions of Fatherhood*. Beverly Hills: Sage.

Perlmutter, F.D. 1985. "Ethical Issues in Family Mediation: A Social Perspective." *Mediation Quarterly* 8.

Pleck, J.H. 1984. "The Work-Family Role System." In P.Voydanoff (ed.), *Work and Family*. Palo Alto: Mayfield.

——. 1983. "Husbands' Paid Work and Family Roles: Current Research Issues." In H. Lopata and J.H. Pleck (eds.), *Research in the Interweave of Social Roles: Families and Jobs*. Greenwich, Conn.: JAI.

——. 1979. "Men's Family Work: Three Perspectives and Some New Data." *Family Coordinator* 28(4).

Pleck, J.H., M.E. Lamb, and J.A. Levine. 1986. "Epilog: Facilitating Future Change in Men's Family Roles." *Marriage and Family Review* 9(3-4).

Pleck, J.H., and L. Lang. 1978. *Men's Family Role: Its Nature and Consequences.* Wellesley, Mass: Wellesley College Center for Research on Women.

Pleck, J.H., and M. Rustad. 1981. "Wives' Employment, Role Demands, and Adjustment." Unpublished manuscript. Wellesley, Mass.: Wellesley College Center for Research on Women.

——. 1980. "Husbands' and Wives' Time in Family Work and Paid Work in the 1975-76 Study of Time Use. Unpublished manuscript. Wellesley, Mass.: Wellesley College Center for Research on Women.

Polikoff, N.D. 1982. "Gender and Child Custody Determinations: Exploding the Myths." In I. Diamond (ed.) , *Families, Politics, and Public Policies: A Feminist Dialogue on Women and the State.* New York: Longman.

Quarm, D. 1984. "Sexual Inequality: The High Cost of Leaving Parenting to Women." In K.M. Borman, D. Quarm, and S. Gideonse (eds.), *Women in the Workplace: Effects on Families.* Norwood, N.J.: Ablex.

Quinn, R., and G. Staines. 1978. *The 1977 Quality of Employment Survey.* Ann Arbor, Mich.: Institute for Social Research.

Raschke, H.J. 1977. "The Role of Social Participation in Postseparation and Postdivorce Adjustments." *Journal of Divorce* 1(2).

Ricci, I. 1985." Mediator's Notebook: Reflections on Promoting Equal Empowerment and Entitlements for Women." *Journal of Divorce* 8(3).

——. 1980. *Mom's House, Dad's House.* New York: MacMillan.

Richards, M.P.M. 1989. "Joint Custody Revisited." *Family Law* 19.

——. 1982a. "How Should We Approach the Study of Fathers?" In L. McKee and M. O'Brien (eds.), *The Father Figure.* London: Tavistock.

——. 1982b. "Post-Divorce Arrangements for Children: A Psychological Perspective." *Journal of Social Welfare Law 69.* London: Sweet and Maxwell.

Richards, M.P.M. and M. Dyson. 1982. *Separation, Divorce, and the Development of Children: A Review.* London: Department of Health and Social Security.

Ricks, S.S. 1984. "Determining Child Custody: Trends, Factors, and Alternatives." *Conciliation Courts Review* 22(1).

Rifkin, E. 1984. "Mediation from a Feminist Perspective: Promise and Problems." *Law and Inequality* 21(2).

Robinson, B.E. 1979. "Men Caring for the Young: An Androgynous Perspective." *Family Coordinator* 28(4).

Robinson, M. 1991. Family Transformation through Divorce and Remarriage. London: Routledge.

Roman, M. 1986. "Joint Custody Fathers: An Update." In J.W. Jacobs (ed.), *Divorce and Fatherhood.* Los Angeles: American Psychiatric Press.

Roman, M., and W. Haddad. 1978. *The Disposable Parent.* New York: Holt, Rinehart and Winston.

Rosenthal, K.M., and H.T. Keshet. 1981. *Fathers Without Partners: A Study of Fathers and the Family After Marital Separation.* Totowa, N.J.: Rowan and Littlefield.

Rossi, A. 1983. "Transition to Parenthood." In A. Skolnick and J. Skolnick (eds.), *Family in Transition.* Boston: Little, Brown.

Rotundo, E.A. 1985. "American Fatherhood: A Historical Perspective." *American Behavioral Scientist* 29.

Russell, G. 1983. *The Changing Role of Fathers.* Milton Keynes: Open University Press.

Rutter, M. 1972. *Maternal Deprivation Reassessed.* Harmondsworth: Penguin.

Saposnek, D.T. 1983. *Mediating Child Custody Disputes.* San Franciso: Jossey-Bass.

Scanzoni, J. 1979. "An Historical Perspective on Husband-Wife Bargaining Power and Marital Dissolution." In G. Levinger and O.C. Moles (eds.), *Divorce and Separation.* New York: Basic Books.

Scher, M. 1981. "Men in Hiding: A Challenge for the Counsellor."*The Personnel and Guidance Journal* (December).

Schuman, D.C. 1981. "Psychiatric Aspects of Custody Loss." In I.R. Stuart and L.E. Abt (eds.), *Children of Separation and Divorce.* New York: Van Nostrand Reinhold.

Seagull, A.A., and E.A. Seagull. 1977. "The Non-Custodial Fathers' Relationship to his Child: Conflicts and Solutions." *Journal of Clinical Child Psychology* 2.

Search, G. 1983. *Surviving Divorce.* Sevenoaks, Kent: New English Library.

Segal, L. 1990. *Slow Motion: Changing Masculinities, Changing Men.* London: Virago Press.

Sev'er, A. 1992.*Women and Divorce in Canada.* Toronto: Canadian Scholars' Press.

Shiller, V.M. 1984. Joint Custody: An Appraisal. Doctoral dissertation, Yale University.

Sideris, N. 1988. "Divorce Mediation: Must It Be Voluntary?" *Conciliation Courts Review* 26(2).

Smart, L.S. 1977. "An Application of Erikson's Theory to the Recovery-From-Divorce Process." *Journal of Divorce* 1(1).

Smith, E.J. 1981. "Non-Judicial Resolution of Custody and Visitation Disputes." In H.H. Irving (ed.), *Family Law.* Toronto: Carswell.

Spanier, G.B., and R.F. Castro. 1979. "Adjustment to Separation and Divorce: A Qualitative Analysis." In G. Levinger and O.C. Moles (eds.), *Divorce and Separation.* New York: Basic Books.

Sprenkle, D.H., and C.L. Storm. 1983. "Divorce Therapy Outcome Research: A Substantive and Methodological Review." *Journal of Marital and Family Therapy* 9(3).

Statistics Canada. 1990. *Women in Canada: A Statistical Report.* Second edition. Ottawa: Minister of Supply and Services.

———. 1988. *Canadian Social Trends.* Ottawa: Minister of Supply and Services.

Stevens, J.H., Jr., and J. Mathews, eds. 1978. *Mother-Child, Father-Child Relations.* Washington: National Association for the Education of Young Children.

Stuart, I.R. and L.F. Abt, eds. 1981. *Children of Separation and Divorce.* New York: Van Nostrand Reinhold.

Trost, M.R., S.L. Brayer, and R. Schoeneman. 1988. "Mandatory Mediation: Encouraging Results for the Court System." *Conciliation Courts Review* 26(2).

Veroff, J., and S. Feld, 1970. *Marriage and Work in America.* New York: Van Nostrand Reinhold.

Voydanoff, P., ed. 1984. *Work and Family: Changing Roles of Men and Women.* Palo Alto: Mayfield.

Walker, K., and M. Woods. 1976. *Time Use: A Measure of Household Production of Family Goods and Services.* Washington: American Home Economics Association.

Wallerstein, J.S., and J. Kelly. 1980. *Surviving the Breakup: How Children and Parents Cope with Divorce.* New York: Basic Books.

Warner, R.L. 1986. "Alternative Strategies for Measuring Household Division of Labor." *Journal of Family Issues* 7.

Warshak, R.A., and J.W. Santrock. 1983. "The Impact of Divorce in Father-Custody and Mother-Custody Homes: The Child's Perspective." In L.A. Kurdek (ed.), *Children and Divorce: New Directions for Child Development.* San Francisco: Jossey-Bass.

Weinraub, M. 1978. "Fatherhood: The Myth of the Second-Class Parent." In J.H. Stevens Jr. and M. Mathews (eds.), *Mother-Child, Father-Child Relations.* Washington: National Association for the Education of Young Children.

Weiss, R.S. 1979a. "The Emotional Impact of Marital Separation." In G. Levinger and O.C. Moles (eds.), *Divorce and Separation.* New York: Basic Books.

——. 1979b. "Growing Up a Little Faster: The Experience of Growing Up in a Single-Parent Household." *Journal of Social Issues* 35(4).

——. 1979c. "Issues in the Adjudication of Custody when Parents Separate." In G. Levinger and O.C. Moles (eds.), *Divorce and Separation.* New York: Basic Books.

Weitzman, L. 1985. *The Divorce Revolution: Social and Unintended Consequences.* New York: Free Press.

White, S.W., and B.L. Bloom. 1981. "Factors Related to the Adjustment of Divorcing Men." *Family Relations* (30).

Williams, F.S. 1986. "A Father's Post-Divorce Struggle for Parental Identity." In J.W. Jacobs (ed.), *Divorce and Fatherhood.* Los Angeles: American Psychiatric Press.

——. 1983. "What Can Judges and Mediators Do to Ameliorate the Effects of Divorce on Parents and Children?" *Family Law News* 6.

Wilson, S.J. 1991. *Women, Families, and Work.* Third edition. Toronto: McGraw-Hill.

Winn, D. 1986. *Men in Divorce.* London: Piatkus.

Wiseman, R.S. 1975. "Crisis Theory and the Process of Divorce." *Social Casework* 56.

Wolchik, S.A., S.L. Braver, and I.N. Sandler. 1985. "Maternal Versus Joint Custody: Children's Postseparation Experiences and Adjustment." *Journal of Clinical Child Psychology* 14(1).

Wylder, J. 1982. "Including the Divorced Father in Family Therapy." *Social Work* 27(6).

Zemmelman, S.E., S.B. Steinman, and T.M. Knoblauch. 1987. "A Model Project on Joint Custody for Families Undergoing Divorce." *Social Work* 32(1).